Clean Your Record and Own a Gun

By
William Rinehart

Desert Publications
El Dorado, AR 71731-1751

Clear Your Record and Own a Gun

© 1995 by William Rinehart

Published by
Desert Publications
P.O. Box 1751
El Dorado, AR 71731-1751
501-862-2077

ISBN 0-87947-095-X
10 9 8 7 6 5 4 3 2 1
Printed in U. S. A.

Desert Publication is a division of
The DELTA GROUP, Ltd.
Direct all inquires & orders to the above address.

All rights reserved. Except for use in a review, no portion of this book may be reproduced by any means known or unknown without the express written permission of the publisher.

Neither the author nor the publisher assumes any responsibility for the use or misuse of the information contained in this book.

INTRODUCTION

Dedication

To Maria, the most patient woman in the world and Rosa, my nine going on eighteeen year old daughter, Senator Max Jordan, Doug Ashy, Sr., and Reverend Don Ross.

Clear Your Record and Own a Gun

Introduction

I can remember when I was eight years old, how impatiently I waited for my father to get his first retirement check. He had promised to buy me a B. B. gun. I checked the mailbox every time I got off the school bus, and suddenly one day it was there. Within hours I had in my inexperienced hands a Daisy Red Ryder Lever-action, magazine-loading, plastic stock B. B. Rifle. I became an expert at popping tin cans like they were 'the bad guys'. My dad supervised me for the first month or so.

Then, when I was twelve, and still living in the woods of southeastern Ohio, I was given the chore of carrying ice cold spring water from the little shallow pool far back in the hollow between the hills behind our house. It was hard work, the bucket was heavy, but I imagined myself as a hunter and the bucket was my weapon. The day finally came when my dad came with me, but he carried the bucket, and I carried the old .20 gauge shotgun he kept behind his bedroom door. He had taught me how to carry it, how to load it, how to aim, and where not to point it.

Our dog chased a squirrel into a tree. My dad took a green briar and pulled him out, telling me to shoot when the squirrel was high in the tree. I let him climb to the top, and when he jumped from that tree to another, I shot him in mid-air. It was my first experience with a real gun. I was so excited I was jumping. We ate the squirrel. When I was a little older, my dad taught me about rifles, about how they were more dangerous, how they had much longer range than a shotgun, about how to never shoot at anything unless I knew what was behind it for over a mile. We had an old bolt-action single shot Remington, .22– I wore it out. "Barking" squirrels, that game of not shooting at the squirrel directly, but hitting the limb he was on became a favorite game. I had grown to love hunting, and my family knew it. But I had been trained.

By the time I graduated from high school as the youngest in our family of twelve, there were shotguns, rifles, bows, sling-

shots, and pistols in our house. We always ate what we killed–
sometimes it was the only source of meat we had. But each of us
had been taught how to handle guns. They were a tool, a source
of pleasure, a necessity in that part of the country.

Then came the Army; it taught me to use these tools for other
purposes, but they still taught me the responsibility that went
with them. I had to qualify with numerous firearms– the old M-
1, the M-14, the M-16, the .30 caliber machine gun, the .50 caliber
machine gun, the 3.5 rocket launcher, the B. A. R. (Browning
Automatic Rifle), the .45 caliber automatic pistol, and others. I
was in the Combat Engineers, but I was also assigned as a guard
at the post stockade.

Guns were an everyday thing in my life for many years–
until 1973, when I made a mistake, and the law called it a crime.
No guns were involved in what I did; suffice it to say that it was
a moment of inebriated stupidity. But I now had a felony
criminal record and was not allowed to carry, buy, sell, trade,
hunt with or own any kind of weapon. That fact, given that I had
grown up around guns, almost killed me. My hunting days
were over. Friends asked me to go with them, and when I
begged off, I couldn't tell them why without revealing my
stupidity. There were many embarrassing monments, for them
and for me.

I vowed to regain that right to bear arms, if for nothing else
to get my pride back. And I worked at it. Hard. From 1973 to
1983, I picked up another felony, many misdemeanors, and had
my work cut out for me. Now, in October, 1994, I can legally
carry, buy, sell, trade, own, hunt with, borrow, lend, or do
anything else I used to do with guns before 1973. And the Brady
Bill or the Crime Bill had nothing whatsoever to do with it . It
was a bit of work. I hope my work pays off for you.

Introduction

This book contains methods for restoring the right to bear arms in several jurisdictions, federal, state, and within some states. By no means does it propose to contain all of the ways that rights can be restored. Other than the federal methods, it is a guide to be used in and among the several states that do have statutes for the relief from the disability of the loss of the right to bear arms by reason of a criminal conviction. The federal statutes must stand as they are written.

Upon purchase and/or use of this material, you will notice that the laws in each state are very specific, and they tell you exactly what to do and where to do it. Whereas some states have laws for expungement, some do not. As stated by the Supreme Court, there are even some states that do not have any procedure for the restoring of civil rights once a conviction has been recorded.

Among the several ways to restore your rights are expungement (erasure of the record), pardon, sealing of the record, dismissal of the case, having a relief from disability granted, getting permission from a local law enforcement officer, and executive pardon from the president which restores your rights everywhere. This is a book of ideas, of what you need, where to go for the material you need, and what to do with it when you have it. With a little research, you can do all of your

Introduction

own work. It's not as difficult as people would have you believe, it just looks that way.

First, look in the criminal law codes of your own state, and those books are all over the place, even public libraries. Turn to the back under that part marked Words & Phrases. Then look for the key words, expungement, pardon, dismissal, sealing of records, relief from disability, etc. You will need a copy of your minutes, (that document that has your case number, and sentence on it, as well as the date of the offense and who the presiding judge was.)

With the minutes and law book in hand, you can start clearing your record on the spot-by reading exactly how your state wants it done.

There are many mentions of where to find free help in this book, such as legal aid society, indigent defendant's office, probation/parole office, clerks of court, law schools, judges, and more. The easiest way to begin for the entities not covered in this book? Pick up your phone, call the clerk of court, criminal division, where your record is now, and ask if that court has a method of restoring your rights of citizenship. If they don't know, ask for someone who does. There is a way, and you can find it, believe me.

Frustration and confusion are not out of the question, and I can say that from experience. But, don't quit! It may take a while, but it'll all come together. Dig out what you need, put it to use, and you will be surprised at what you can do on your own.

Use this book. It's full of ideas on how and where to go to get things done. You can regain your right to bear arms.

Contents

Chapter		Page
One	Owning Guns	1
Two	Opportunities/Advantages	5
Three	All State's Gun Laws	9
Four	Federal Jurisdictions Firearm Rights Recovery	27
Five	California Firearm Rights Recovery	49
Six	Louisiana Firearms Rights Recovery	69
Seven	Ohio Firearms Rights Recovery	91
Eight	Get Your Case in Court	109
Nine	Influence, How to Use It	117
Ten	Filing Your Papers for Free	121
	Epilog	123
	Glossary	125
	Sources	129

Chapter 1
Owning Guns

Some people have asked why, after reading *How To Clear Your Criminal Record*, I would want to write a book entitled *Clear Your Record and Own A Gun*. They know, as well as I do, that if I don't have a record I can own weapons. But, just 'clearing the record' wasn't enough.

It's hard to explain.

On a hot August night, in 1973, after a friend and I had worked all day on a house roof getting the eaves ready to paint, we decided we had earned ourselves a cold beer. We went to our apartment, changed clothes, and drank a couple of six packs apiece. At that time I wouldn't have admitted that I was an alcoholic, but I was.

We decided to go out for a while, but we had been watching television until it was very late. All the bars were closed. I wanted something to drink: bad. We decided in our drunken stupor to break into a bar and take nothing but a couple of bottles of whiskey. I had never before had any kind of criminal record.

After banging on the plywood cover of a window of a closed bar, the window was slid back and shots were fired at us. I ducked and laid down on the sidewalk. After we were arrested, the police ran a check on my blood/alcohol level. They said I should have been in a deep coma or dead. We were charged with breaking and entering into an inhabited dwelling which at that time carried 5-30 years in Ohio, and because I still had the knife I had been using to scrape the paint from the roof in my back pocket, a charge of Carrying A Concealed Weapon was added. CCW, in Ohio, at that time, carried 1-15 years. At the outside, I was looking at 45 years in the penitentiary. At that time, I was only 28 years old. (Since then, a full pardon, and relief from disability has been granted for those charges).

Then, on a hot May evening, in southern Louisiana, in 1983, (and still a practicing alcoholic), another young friend and I were out drinking-but he was out stealing. He came back to where I was waiting for him with a little AWOL bag with things he had stolen. Among them were a temporary license plate, some marijuana seeds and stems, and an old .22 Caliber revolver. He was playing Wyatt Earp with the gun when it went off, firing into the night sky. I took the gun away from him, and we tried to sell it to get some more booze. I was still carrying the little bag he had stolen with the gun still in it when we were caught by the police. Again, I was charged with burglary-of two cars, and carrying a concealed weapon. (I believe that's called 'left holding the bag'.) But, since that has happened, that record has been expunged twice, (erased), and granted two full pardons.

Then there was the case of going to use the restroom in a Houston, Texas bar and a man called 'Doc' pulled a gun on me while I was zipping my pants. He said he was going to blow my head off-I told him to hurry up, my beer was getting warm. I was out the door and back at the bar talking to the bartender before he had a chance to know what happened. 'Doc' was thrown out of the bar, leaving his gun with the bartender. Of course, I was literally hung from a ceiling beam in Odessa, Texas, after being shot with a pellet gun several times while a punk kid watched me die. But, I didn't die. The 'hanging rope', my own belt, broke.

And, of course, there was the time when my brother Calvin shot my brother Dan with his .12 gauge shotgun, and my dad grabbed my .20 gauge for a standoff until the sheriff got there to straighten things out. Calvin went to prison, Dan never forgot.

My brother Pete used to walk around with a .22 pistol strapped to his leg, until he sold it for some quick cash.

Then there was the time when Sheriff Steele, a good and close friend of my dad's, was killed while trying to serve a warrant. Everybody in Vinton County, Ohio, who was big enough to carry a gun went out looking for the killer–myself included. He was caught on an old logging road, without a shot being fired.

My father was a cop. But he was more than that, he was a moral human being. He was at one time in the FBI, and was a part of that group that was sent to intercede in the West Virginia Clan War between the Hatfields and the McCoys. He was also a security officer at Wright-Patterson Air Force Base, a private investigator, and finally, a tower guard at the Ohio Penitentiary in Columbus. He wore a gun most of his life.

I relate this to you for one reason-I was trained to respect weapons-not abuse them. I was trained to think of them as a tool, to be used to do a job, not commit crimes or intimidate others. In the hands of responsible people, there can be no greater source of security. Never in my life have I pointed a gun at anyone. I hope I never have to. And, yes, I have worked as a prison guard at the Louisiana State Prison, at Angola, and at Hunt Corrections Center in St. Gabriel, Louisiana as an armed tower guard since I had the criminal record. Impossible? No.

The point? The bottom line? Cut to the "chase"? If you want to regain your right to bear arms for all the "wrong" reasons, take heed-it will catch up with you in the long run.

Chapter 2
Opportunities \ Advantages

When you are dealing with the legal aspects of practically anything, you end up playing politics. It cannot be avoided. Law and politics are so intertwined that it's sometimes hard to tell the difference. And, as many of us are not schooled in law and politics, getting lost in the shuffle of the 'old boy networks' of local and state politics is exceptionally easy. If lawyers are chosen to try to regain your right to bear arms for you, there are definite advantages. One of these is that they are already within the structure of law and politics that you need to navigate to get what you're after. Put another way, they know all the right people. Most of us don't just hire any lawyer when we need one, we hire one that knows the laws, the judge, the area of law our case deals with, etc. People accused of crimes hire criminal lawyers. People wanting to sue someone hire a civil lawyer. The more expensive they are, the more contacts they are likely to have. It's that simple.

But, in dealing with the restoration of the right to bear arms, there is no division – you are dealing with a right that is revoked by criminal law, period. The problem is, that same right can be restored by civil law and civil litigation. It gets confusing.

So, do you hire a criminal law attorney, or a civil litigation lawyer? Who knows the most? Who costs the most? Who can get the job done?

You.

Lawyers would like for you to believe that you can do nothing without them. They make their money that way-by telling you that you cannot do it by yourself. They have told me that for years. I almost believed them. Almost.

For you to get your right to own, carry, buy, sell, trade, transport, receive, hunt with, and protect yourself with weapons, the person best qualified for the job is you.

Without a lawyer. The fewer people that know what you are trying to do, the better. Discretion is required, not preferred. The quieter you go about your business of getting your rights back, the better off you are.

Why? Well, for one thing, you don't need to advertise to anyone that you don't already have the right to bear arms-that you have a criminal record, that you made a mistake. Hiring an attorney allows several things; first, you have to go to or call an attorney. In doing so, before you can talk to him/her, someone will screen you-and they will ask you why you want to see this attorney. If you refuse to tell them, they won't let you see the lawyer. This person is generally a receptionist, or secretary, or paralegal. This individual is not legally bound to confidentiality, and could tell anyone that you came into his/her office looking for a way to get back your rights to get a gun. Office gossip goes to coffee shops and lunch counters, and then to the street.

By the time you see the lawyer, your request might be already on the street. Suppose this lawyer hasn't the time or inclination to see you? You have to repeat the whole thing, and eventually, word of your wanting to restore your rights will be spread around-to people that didn't even know you had a criminal record. Legal personnel are not as secretive as you might think. I know.

Then, of course, the lawyer you hire has to go to the courthouse records to look up your crime and make copies.

The courthouse people are not known to be that respectful of your privacy either. Ask O. J. Simpson. The clerks there will soon know what you're trying to do.

Then, of course, if it was a secretary instead of the paralegal in your lawyer's office that you talked to in the beginning, the paralegal will know of you when he/she starts preparing your file. They, too, have been known to not respect total privacy.

By the time your right to bear arms ever gets to a courthouse in front of a judge, just about everybody knows who you are, where you work, who your wife or girlfriend/boyfriend is, what's in your criminal record, what you did, when and where you did it, and the consequences. Unless you can afford that kind of gossip, you need to know that you can do it yourself!

Expungements, (erasing the record), dismissals of prosecution(s), (dropping the charges), corrections of records, pardons, Motions For Restoration of all Civil Rights, Motions for relief from disabilities, full pardons, motions for sealing of your criminal records, etc., are all just a bunch of words put properly together on sheets of paper, taken to a court house and filed or mailed to a pardon board. It doesn't take a rocket scientist or brain surgeon to put words on sheets of paper.

You made a mistake. Courts make mistakes. But, seldom do courts of law have to pay for their mistakes. No one calls their mistakes to anyone's attention. Actually, it gives you an advantage.

Let's say that you filed a motion for expungement in a court. It was denied because the assistant D. A. in your case simply didn't want to erase your record. They have that kind of clout-they can "just say no", and you're done. The judge just says, "sorry, there's nothing I can do if the prosecutor doesn't agree". Are you finished? Do you just hang your tail between your legs and crawl out of the courtroom?

No! You thank the judge and leave the courtroom. You keep your motion to expunge. You wait until either the next election, or until that particular assistant D.A. leaves his/her office. Then under a new judge, or a new assistant D.A., you re-file your Motion To Expunge without anyone telling the judge they're against it. (I was denied the first time–but I saw my assistant D.A. on television, in a position that had nothing whatsoever to do with the District Attorney's office. I called, and sure enough, she had quit. I immediately re-filed my Expungement, and i was granted). It was simply a matter of keeping my eyes ope and my mouth shut.

The same goes with pardons. If you apply for a full pardon with restoration of right to bear arms, and you're turned down, it's not the end of the road. New governors get elected, and replace old pardon boards with new ones–just about every four years. Just reapply every year until you have what you want. They do respect persistence (I know, I applied three times before I got my pardon–without the right to bear arms–then reapplied under a new governor, and got the right to bear arms back).

Same with relief from disability, (the disability is the right to bear arms), or any other thing you do. Just keep doing it!!! It will come.

Keep up with elections, local and state. Keep up with your local politicians-and put bumper stickers on your car. Make a campaign donation, go to rallies, make some influential friends. It can't hurt. Most importantly, keep your eyes open for the chance you need to get what you want, then go after it. **DO NOT HIRE A LAWYER.**

Chapter 3
All State's Gun Laws

Background checks, waiting periods, licenses, permits, registrations, record of sales to police, state carrying a concealed weapon laws, prohibited firearms laws, ownership I. D. cards, constitutional provisions, and state firearms preemption laws for each state are charted on pages 11, 12, and 13 in this chapter.

[Source: U. S. Department of Justice, Office of Justice Programs, Bureau of Justice Statistics; SOURCEBOOK as provided by the National Rifle Association of America.]

The following charts appear on pages 142 and 143 of the SOURCEBOOK. As an example on how to read the chart for your particular state, I will use the three states included in this book, California, Louisiana, and Ohio.

Using California first, I can see that: no, California does not have the instant background check, the federal waiting period does not apply, the state waiting period for both a handgun or long gun is fifteen days, no license or permit is needed for the purchase, no registration, yes, a copy of the sale is sent to the police, yes, there is a concealed carrying law, (and upon further inspection, I can see that Y^f means permits are sharply restrictive, difficult to obtain, if obtainable at all), carrying a gun openly is prohibited if it is loaded, 'assault weapons' are banned, no I. D. cards, no constitutional provision, and that some local restrictions are more restrictive than state laws.

Looking next at Louisiana: permits are issued at the discretion of local law enforcement (see Louisiana in this book), no firearms prohibited, and local laws may be more restrictive than state law.

For Ohio, under the same table of laws: no instant background check, yes, the federal waiting period applies, the state waiting period on handguns is in certain cities or counties, license in certain cities or counties, record of sale sent to police in certain cities or counties, permits are very hard to get, can get permits to carry openly in certain cities or counties, 'assault weapons' banned, does have constitutional provisions, and not preempted by state law.

As can be seen, there are major differences in just these three states. Be sure to look at your own state laws prior to the use of this manual.

For your convenience, the following pages show the tables as well as tables that tell you how many people have firearms in their homes, attitudes toward laws covering the sales of firearms, attitudes towards the registration of handguns, attitudes toward banning the possession of handguns except by the police or other authorized person, attitudes toward a law requiring a police permit prior to gun purchase, attitudes toward a national seven day waiting period for buying a handgun, selected gun control measures, attitudes towards proposed gun control measures, and more.

All State's Gun Laws

Statutory restrictions on the purchase, carrying, and ownership of firearms

By State, 1994

State	Instant background check	Federal waiting period applies[a]	State waiting period (in days) Handgun	State waiting period (in days) Long gun	License or permit to purchase Handgun	License or permit to purchase Long gun	Registration Handgun	Registration Long gun	Record of sales sent to police	State concealed carry law	Carrying openly prohibited	Certain firearms prohibited	Ownership licensing or identification cards	Constitutional provision	State firearms preemption law[b]
Alabama		Y	2						Y	Y[c]	Y[d]			Y	Y
Alaska		Y								Y[e]				Y	Y
Arizona		Y								Y[c]				Y	Y
Arkansas		Y								Y[f]				Y	
California	Y		15	15					Y	Y[f]	Y[g]	Y[i]			Y[k]
Colorado	Y Y		14[j]	14[j]						Y[f]	Y[h]	Y[i]		Y	Y[k]
Connecticut	Y Y								Y	Y[c]	Y			Y	Y[k]
Delaware			3							Y[e]	Y			Y	Y
Florida		Y[l]	(m)							Y[c]	Y			Y	Y
Georgia			(n)	(n)	Y		Y			Y[c]	Y	Y[i]		Y	Y
Hawaii	Y		3[c]	1[c]	Y[o]		Y[p]			Y[f]		Y[i]	Y[o]	Y	Y
Idaho			7		Y[n] Y[E]	Y	Y[p]	Y[p]	Y	Y[c]				Y	Y[q]
Illinois							Y[E]			Y[c]	Y[E]			Y	Y
Indiana		Y Y	(m)						Y	Y[f]	Y	Y[i]		Y	Y
Iowa		Y Y Y Y	(m)						Y	Y[f]	Y			Y	Y
Kansas		Y Y	7	7[r]	Y	Y			Y	Y[c]	Y[d]		Y	Y	Y[k]
Kentucky			(n)	(n)	Y	Y[r]			Y	Y[f]	Y[d]			Y	Y
Louisiana			7		Y		Y[s]			Y[f]	Y			Y	Y
Maine		Y[l]			Y					Y[c]			Y	Y	Y
Maryland		Y	(n)						Y	Y[c]					Y
Massachusetts			(n)							Y[f]					Y
Michigan		Y					Y[m]		Y	Y[c]				Y	Y
Minnesota															
Mississippi	Y								Y	Y[c]				Y	Y
Missouri															
Montana															
Nebraska															
Nevada															
New Hampshire															

11

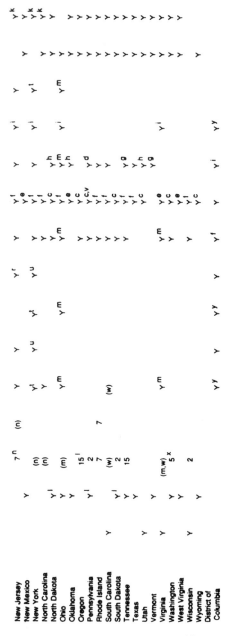

Footnotes for data are on the next page.

All State's Gun Laws

Note: These data were compiled by the National Rifle Association of America, Institute for Legislative Action. In addition to State laws, the purchase, sale, and in certain circumstances, the possession and interstate transportation of firearms are regulated by the Federal Gun Control Act of 1968 as amended by the Firearms Owners' Protection Act. Also, cities and localities may have their own firearms ordinances in addition to Federal and State laws. A "Y" in the table indicates that the attribute is present. However, many qualifications may apply. The Source notes that State firearms laws are subject to frequent change. State and local statutes and ordinances, as well as local law enforcement authorities, should be consulted for full text and meaning of statutory provisions.

A long gun is a rifle or shotgun. The Source defines "constitutional provision" by citing Article 1, Section 15 of the Connecticut State Constitution as an example of the basic feature contained in the constitutions of many States. It reads: "Every citizen has a right to bear arms in defense of himself and the State."

[a] The Federal 5-day waiting period for handgun purchases applies to States that don't have instant background checks, waiting period requirements, or licensing procedures exempting them from the Federal requirement. Application of the Federal waiting period is determined from the Bureau of Alcohol, Tobacco and Firearms.
[b] A State firearms preemption law proscribes the existence of a local law or ordinance more restrictive than a State law governing firearms.
[c] Least restrictive: most have "shall issue" permit systems.
[d] Carrying handgun openly in a motor vehicle requires a license.
[e] Moderately restrictive: permit issuance subject to discretion of local law enforcement, or permits are unavailable and concealed carry is prohibited in some circumstances.
[f] Sharply restrictive: permits are difficult to obtain or unavailable entirely.
[g] Arkansas prohibits carrying a firearm "with a purpose to employ it as a weapon against a person"; Tennessee prohibits carrying "with the intent to go armed"; Vermont prohibits carrying "with the intent or purpose of injuring another."
[h] Loaded.
[i] California, Connecticut, New Jersey, New York City, other local jurisdictions in New York, and several cities in Ohio have banned "assault weapons." Some Ohio cities also forbid the possession and sale of handguns with a certain magazine capacity. In Illinois, Chicago and certain other cities have banned handguns and "assault weapons." Maryland has banned several small, low-caliber, inexpensive handguns and "assault pistols." Hawaii has banned "assault pistols." Virginia has banned Street Sweeper shotguns and the District of Columbia has banned handguns and semi-automatic firearms with the ability to use a magazine holding more than 12 rounds. (In some cases, individuals are allowed to keep any banned firearm possessed prior to the effective date of the gun-ban law, with certain restrictions.)
[j] Holders of carry permits are exempt from the waiting period. A hunting license provides exemption on long guns only.
[k] Preemption through judicial ruling, not statute. Local regulation may be instituted in Massachusetts and North Carolina, but it must be ratified by legislative action. Waiting period does not apply to persons holding valid permits/licenses to carry handguns issued within 5 years of proposed purchase.
[m] In certain cities or counties.
[n] The permit-to-purchase system constitutes a waiting period for first-time gun buyers in the following States: Illinois, Nebraska, Massachusetts, Missouri, New Jersey, New York, and North Carolina. In Iowa, permits-to-purchase are good only after three days from date of issue. Hawaii's permit-to-purchase system constitutes a 14 to 20-day waiting period for first-time gun buyers as the law requires law enforcement to hold the permit-to-purchase for 14 days and no longer than 20 days. Subsequent permits may be granted in less time.
[o] Handguns prohibited in Evanston, Oak Park, Morton Grove, Winnetka, Wilmette, and Highland Park.
[p] Chicago only.
[q] Except Gary and East Chicago.
[r] Applies to "military style" semi-automatics. In New Jersey, applies only to firearms lawfully possessed prior to 1990 ban. In Minnesota, applies to a specific list of 17 semi-automatic firearms.
[s] Handguns must be presented to the city chief of police or county sheriff to obtain a certificate of inspection.
[t] New York's permit system combines purchase, possession, and carry in a single permit. New York City requires a permit for all guns.
[u] New York City only.
[v] Except Philadelphia.
[w] Handgun purchases limited to 1 per 30-day period, with certain exceptions.
[x] Can be extended by police to 30 days under some circumstances. Non-driver's license holders must wait 90 days.
[y] Applies only to handguns registered and re-registered prior to the District of Columbia's 1977 handgun "ban," and to all long guns. No additional handguns may be acquired by District of Columbia residents.

Source: Table provided to SOURCEBOOK staff by the National Rifle Association of America, Institute for Legislative Action.

CLEAR YOUR RECORD AND OWN A GUN

Table 2.56

Respondents reporting a firearm in their home

By demographic characteristics, United States, selected years 1973-93

Question: "Do you happen to have in your home (or garage) any guns or revolvers?"

(Percent reporting having any guns)

	1973	1974	1976	1977	1980	1982	1984	1985	1987	1988	1989	1990	1991	1993
National	47 %	46 %	47 %	51 %	48 %	45 %	45 %	44 %	46 %	40 %	46 %	43 %	40 %	42 %
Sex														
Male	53	51	52	55	56	54	53	54	51	50	55	53	50	53
Female	43	42	43	47	41	39	40	36	43	33	39	34	32	34
Race														
White	49	48	58	53	50	48	48	46	49	43	50	45	42	45
Black/other	38	32	37	34	29	30	30	29	33	28	23	29	29	26
Education														
College	45	42	44	45	41	39	42	40	43	37	41	37	34	38
High school	50	48	50	54	51	51	48	49	50	43	51	47	46	46
Grade school	44	49	42	51	51	41	43	38	44	39	46	47	39	47
Occupation														
Professional/business	48	45	46	48	45	42	42	40	45	39	46	38	35	38
Clerical	42	43	40	49	45	39	41	40	45	37	37	38	35	36
Manual	48	48	48	52	48	49	48	48	46	41	52	50	47	51
Farmer	83	79	62	66	81	77	84	78	75	82	87	83	56	68
Income[a]														
$50,000 and over	X	X	X	X	X	X	X	X	X	X	X	X	X	49
$30,000 to $49,999	X	X	X	X	X	X	X	X	X	X	X	X	X	48
$20,000 to $29,999	X	X	X	X	X	X	X	X	X	X	X	X	X	44
Under $20,000	X	X	X	X	X	X	X	X	X	X	X	X	X	32
Age														
18 to 20 years	50	34	38	54	48	51	44	39	43	33	35	40	22	48
21 to 29 years	43	48	45	45	48	41	37	40	35	34	33	34	36	38
30 to 49 years	51	49	52	55	50	51	48	48	51	42	48	46	40	44
50 years and older	46	44	44	49	46	44	49	44	47	42	50	42	42	42
Region[b]														
Northeast	22	27	29	32	27	32	32	28	31	25	32	30	28	X
Midwest	51	49	48	53	52	48	44	48	46	41	46	44	42	X
South	62	59	60	62	59	52	52	53	55	47	53	52	50	X
West	47	42	44	46	44	47	49	40	47	42	48	39	32	X
Religion														
Protestant	56	52	53	57	56	52	52	50	52	46	53	48	46	47
Catholic	35	37	36	39	36	36	34	35	36	31	36	36	30	36
Jewish	14	7	26	17	6	11	22	9	25	0	18	6	10	9
None	32	40	43	50	39	37	36	44	39	41	36	34	31	37
Politics														
Republican	53	49	50	56	53	50	56	47	51	46	50	48	42	51
Democrat	44	45	45	49	46	44	42	47	44	39	43	40	41	35
Independent	49	47	48	50	47	44	40	39	44	36	46	42	37	42

Note: For a discussion of public opinion survey sampling procedures, see Appendix 5.

[a]Income categories have been revised and therefore are not directly comparable to previous editions of SOURCEBOOK.
[b]Complete data for region were not available for 1993.

Source: Table constructed by SOURCEBOOK staff from data provided by the National Opinion Research Center; data were made available through The Roper Center for Public Opinion Research.

All State's Gun Laws

Table 2.57

Respondents reporting a firearm in their home

By demographic characteristics, United States, 1993

Question: "Do you have a gun in your home?"

	Yes	No
National	49 %	50 %
Sex		
Male	53	45
Female	44	55
Age		
18 to 29 years	45	54
30 to 49 years	46	53
50 to 64 years	58	41
50 years and older	52	46
65 years and older	45	52
Region		
East	34	66
Midwest	45	54
South	62	36
West	49	49
Race		
White	51	48
Black	36	62
Nonwhite[a]	33	64
Education		
College post graduate	36	63
College graduate	41	58
Some college	50	47
No college	51	48
Politics		
Republican	53	46
Democrat	47	52
Independent	45	53
Income		
$50,000 and over	50	48
$30,000 to $49,999	53	47
$20,000 to $29,999	45	55
Under $20,000	41	58
Community		
Urban area	34	65
Suburban area	46	53
Rural area	71	28

Note: The "don't know/refused" category has been omitted; therefore percents may not sum to 100. For a discussion of public opinion survey sampling procedures, see Appendix 5.

[a] Includes black respondents.

Source: Table constructed by SOURCEBOOK staff from data provided by The Gallup Organization, Inc. Reprinted by permission.

Table 2.58

Respondents reporting a firearm in their home

By type of firearm and demographic characteristics, United States, 1993

Question: "Do you happen to have in your home (or garage) any guns or revolvers?" If yes, "Is it a pistol, shotgun, rifle, or what?"

(Percent of respondents reporting having guns)

	Guns in the home			
		Type of firearm		
	Any types	Pistol	Shotgun	Rifle
National	42 %	24 %	27 %	23 %
Sex				
Male	53	28	38	31
Female	34	20	19	17
Race				
White	45	25	29	26
Black/other	26	17	14	9
Education				
College	38	24	22	20
High school	46	25	32	27
Grade school	47	18	30	27
Occupation				
Professional/business	38	22	22	20
Clerical	36	22	23	16
Manual	51	30	33	30
Farmer	68	20	56	48
Income[a]				
$50,000 and over	49	30	30	27
$30,000 to $49,999	48	30	34	29
$20,000 to $29,999	44	27	29	23
Under $20,000	32	13	19	16
Age				
18 to 20 years	48	21	34	21
21 to 29 years	38	21	23	17
30 to 49 years	44	27	27	24
50 years and older	42	22	28	25
Religion				
Protestant	47	27	31	26
Catholic	36	17	23	20
Jewish	9	0	4	4
None	37	24	17	20
Politics				
Republican	51	29	34	28
Democrat	35	18	21	17
Independent	42	26	28	25

Note: For a discussion of public opinion survey sampling procedures, see Appendix 5.

[a] Income categories have been revised and therefore are not directly comparable to previous editions of SOURCEBOOK.

Source: Table constructed by SOURCEBOOK staff from data provided by the National Opinion Research Center; data were made available through The Roper Center for Public Opinion Research.

All State's Gun Laws

Table 2.59

Attitudes toward laws covering the sale of firearms

By demographic characteristics, United States, 1993

Question: "In general, do you feel that the laws covering the sale of firearms should be made more strict, less strict, or kept as they are now?"

	More strict	Less strict	Kept as they are now
National	67 %	7 %	25 %
Sex			
Male	59	10	31
Female	75	4	20
Age			
18 to 29 years	64	11	25
30 to 49 years	71	6	22
50 to 64 years	62	4	33
50 years and older	66	4	28
65 years and older	71	5	22
Region			
East	75	5	19
Midwest	68	8	23
South	65	8	26
West	60	5	33
Race			
White	66	7	26
Black	86	3	11
Nonwhite[a]	80	4	16
Education			
College post graduate	71	6	20
College graduate	73	6	20
Some college	66	7	26
No college	66	7	26
Politics			
Republican	60	7	32
Democrat	80	3	16
Independent	62	9	27
Income			
$50,000 and over	68	6	25
$30,000 to $49,999	64	9	26
$20,000 to $29,999	73	6	20
Under $20,000	69	6	24
Community			
Urban area	76	5	18
Suburban area	68	5	26
Rural area	56	11	33

Note: The "don't know/refused" category has been omitted; therefore percents may not sum to 100. For a discussion of public opinion survey sampling procedures, see Appendix 5.

[a]Includes black respondents.

Source: Table constructed by SOURCEBOOK staff from data provided by The Gallup Organization, Inc. Reprinted by permission.

Table 2.60

Attitudes toward the registration of handguns

United States, selected years 1982-93

Question: "Would you favor or oppose the registration of all handguns?"

	Favor	Oppose	No opinion
1982	66 %	30 %	4 %
1985	70	25	5
1990	81	17	2
1991	80	17	3
1993	81	18	1

Note: For a discussion of public opinion survey sampling procedures, see Appendix 5.

Source: George Gallup, Jr., *The Gallup Poll Monthly*, Report No. 340 (Princeton, NJ: The Gallup Poll, January 1994), p. 20. Reprinted by permission.

Table 2.61

Attitudes toward banning the possession of handguns except by the police and other authorized persons

United States, selected years 1980-93

Question: "Do you think there should or should not be a law that would ban the possession of handguns except by the police and other authorized persons?"

	Should	Should not	Don't know or refused
January 1980	31 %	65 %	4 %
December 1980	38	51	11
April 1981	39	58	3
June 1981	41	54	5
October 1987	42	50	8
September 1990	41	55	4
March 1991	43	53	4
March 1993	42	54	4
December 1993	39	60	1

Note: For a discussion of public opinion survey sampling procedures, see Appendix 5.

Source: George Gallup, Jr., *The Gallup Poll Monthly*, No. 340 (Princeton, NJ: The Gallup Poll, January 1994), p. 22. Reprinted by permission.

All State's Gun Laws

Attitudes toward a law requiring a police permit prior to gun purchase

By demographic characteristics, United States, selected years 1972-93

Question: "Would you favor or oppose a law which would require a person to obtain a police permit before he or she could buy a gun?"

	1972		1973		1974		1975		1976		1977		1980		1982		1984		1985	
	Favor	Oppose	Favor	Oppose	Favor	Oppose	Favor	Oppose	Favor	Oppose	Favor	Oppose	Favor	Oppose	Favor	Oppose	Favor	Oppose	Favor	Oppose
National	70%	27%	74%	25%	75%	24%	74%	24%	72%	27%	72%	26%	69%	29%	72%	26%	70%	27%	72%	26%
Sex																				
Male	61	37	67	32	66	33	66	32	64	35	64	35	63	36	68	31	62	37	65	34
Female	79	17	79	19	83	15	80	17	78	20	78	19	74	23	75	23	76	20	78	20
Race																				
White	70	27	73	25	75	24	73	25	71	27	70	28	68	30	71	27	69	29	72	27
Black/other	69	26	74	24	77	22	81	15	74	24	81	17	81	15	78	19	79	18	76	22
Education																				
College	71	27	76	23	77	22	76	22	71	27	74	25	70	29	76	23	74	25	75	24
High school	72	26	73	25	75	23	74	24	72	27	70	28	69	29	71	27	68	30	71	28
Grade school	66	29	70	27	71	27	68	26	71	28	72	25	70	27	64	30	72	23	69	26
Occupation																				
Professional/business	69	28	71	27	74	25	73	24	74	25	76	23	70	28	75	23	71	27	75	24
Clerical	80	18	78	21	84	16	81	18	78	20	75	22	77	21	77	23	76	23	79	21
Manual	72	26	74	24	74	24	70	27	68	30	68	30	67	32	69	29	68	29	68	31
Farmer	54	44	56	42	52	48	60	33	56	44	66	31	53	47	36	60	48	48	43	57
Income[a]																				
$50,000 and over	X	X	X	X	X	X	X	X	X	X	X	X	X	X	X	X	X	X	X	X
$30,000 to $49,999	X	X	X	X	X	X	X	X	X	X	X	X	X	X	X	X	X	X	X	X
$20,000 to $29,999	X	X	X	X	X	X	X	X	X	X	X	X	X	X	X	X	X	X	X	X
Under $20,000	X	X	X	X	X	X	X	X	X	X	X	X	X	X	X	X	X	X	X	X
Age																				
18 to 20 years	70	27	73	27	75	23	74	26	78	22	69	31	71	29	77	23	71	24	71	29
21 to 29 years	74	24	76	23	77	23	79	19	71	27	72	26	73	27	76	24	73	25	74	25
30 to 49 years	68	29	72	26	76	24	70	27	73	25	70	29	70	29	72	26	70	29	71	28
50 years and older	70	26	74	24	74	24	73	24	70	29	74	24	67	29	69	29	70	26	72	26

Clear Your Record and Own a Gun

Region[b]																				
Northeast	83	16	88	10	88	12	85	13	86	13	85	14	86	13	85	13	80	18	82	17
Midwest	69	27	72	28	77	22	76	22	72	27	67	31	71	27	73	24	70	25	73	25
South	63	33	67	31	70	28	66	30	63	35	69	28	64	34	62	36	66	31	67	32
West	67	32	69	29	66	32	70	29	68	30	68	31	60	38	69	30	67	32	71	29
Religion																				
Protestant	66	31	68	31	71	28	70	27	67	31	67	30	64	34	68	30	66	31	68	30
Catholic	78	19	83	15	85	14	83	15	82	18	80	20	83	16	81	17	79	20	79	20
Jewish	96	4	98	2	98	2	96	4	89	11	89	9	88	12	89	5	93	7	94	6
None	69	29	81	18	70	29	71	28	68	28	73	26	71	28	72	28	78	22	74	26
Politics																				
Republican	70	27	70	28	74	25	74	23	71	27	71	26	64	35	66	33	66	32	70	28
Democrat	72	25	76	22	78	22	77	20	74	25	73	26	74	25	75	24	75	23	74	25
Independent	68	30	73	26	73	25	70	28	69	29	71	28	68	29	72	26	70	28	72	27

Note: The "don't know" category has been omitted; therefore percents may not sum to 100. For a discussion of public opinion survey sampling procedures, see Appendix 5.

[a] Income categories have been revised and therefore are not directly comparable to previous editions of SOURCEBOOK.

[b] Complete data for region were not available for 1993.

Source: Table constructed by SOURCEBOOK staff from data provided by the National Opinion Research Center; data were made available through The Roper Center for Public Opinion Research.

All State's Gun Laws

Table 2.62

Attitudes toward banning the possession of handguns except by the police and other authorized persons

By demographic characteristics, United States, 1993

Question: "Do you think there should or should not be a law that would ban the possession of handguns, except by the police and other authorized persons?"

	Should	Should not
National	39 %	60 %
Sex		
Male	28	71
Female	48	50
Age		
18 to 29 years	39	61
30 to 49 years	38	61
50 to 64 years	34	64
65 years and older	46	51
Region		
East	48	52
Midwest	41	58
South	35	63
West	31	67
Race		
White	36	63
Nonwhite	58	40
Education		
College post graduate	41	58
Total college[a]	38	61
No college	40	58
Politics		
Republican	34	66
Democrat	48	51
Independent	34	64
Income		
$50,000 and over	36	64
$30,000 to $49,999	37	63
$20,000 to $29,999	31	66
Under $20,000	48	51
Community		
Urban area	48	50
Suburban area	37	62
Rural area	28	71

Note: The "don't know/refused" category has been omitted; therefore percents may not sum to 100. For a discussion of public opinion survey sampling procedures, see Appendix 5.

[a] Includes college graduates and persons who attended some college.

Source: George Gallup, Jr., *The Gallup Poll Monthly*, No. 340 (Princeton, NJ: The Gallup Poll, January 1994), p. 22. Reprinted by permission.

Table 2.64

Attitudes toward a national law requiring a 7-day waiting period before purchasing a handgun

By demographic characteristics, United States, 1993

Question: "There is a proposal in Congress called the Brady Bill which would require a 7-day waiting period before a handgun could be purchased, in order to determine whether the prospective buyer has been convicted of a felony, or is mentally ill. Do you favor or oppose this proposal?"

	Favor	Oppose
National	88 %	11 %
Sex		
Male	85	14
Female	90	9
Age		
18 to 29 years	87	13
30 to 49 years	87	13
50 years and older	90	8
Region		
East	93	6
Midwest	84	15
South	85	14
West	90	10
Race		
White	88	11
Black	85	15
Nonwhite[a]	84	16
Education		
College graduate	87	13
College incomplete	92	8
No college	86	13
Politics		
Republican	84	16
Democrat	92	7
Independent	87	12
Income		
$50,000 and over	88	12
$30,000 to $49,999	88	11
$20,000 to $29,999	90	
Under $20,000	86	14
Community		
Urban area	89	11
Suburban area	91	8
Rural area	84	15

Note: The "don't know/refused" category has been omitted; therefore percents may not sum to 100. For a discussion of public opinion survey sampling procedures, see Appendix 5.

[a] Includes black respondents.

Source: Table constructed by SOURCEBOOK staff from data provided by The Gallup Organization, Inc. Reprinted by permission.

All State's Gun Laws

Attitudes toward proposed gun control measures

By demographic characteristics, United States, 1993

Question: "Please tell me whether you would generally favor or oppose each of the following proposals which some people have made to reduce the amount of gun violence: (a) the Brady bill, which requires a five-day waiting period on the purchase of all guns in order to determine whether the prospective buyer has been convicted of a felony; (b) a ban on the manufacture, sale and possession of semi-automatic assault guns, such as the AK-47; (c) prohibiting people with criminal histories from being able to purchase or own guns; (d) requiring people to take safety classes in order to qualify to own a gun; (e) a limit on gun purchases to one per month; (f) a ban on the manufacture and sale of cheap handguns; (g) a very high federal sales tax which would increase the price of bullets for most handguns by 50%; (h) prohibiting people under the age of 18 from being able to purchase a gun."

	Require safety classes		Prohibit purchase by those under 18		Prohibit criminals from purchasing		Brady bill		Ban assault guns		Ban cheap handguns		Limit purchase to one per month		High tax on bullets	
	Favor	Oppose	Favor	Oppose	Favor	Oppose	Favor	Oppose	Favor	Oppose	Favor	Oppose	Favor	Oppose	Favor	Oppose
National	89%	10%	88%	11%	87%	10%	87%	11%	77%	20%	72%	24%	69%	27%	55%	43%
Sex																
Male	89	12	87	12	85	11	84	14	74	28	70	28	66	31	45	53
Female	90	9	89	10	89	9	91	8	80	16	74	20	71	24	63	34
Age																
18 to 29 years	89	11	88	12	84	14	90	9	71	27	67	32	70	27	49	50
30 to 49 years	91	9	91	9	90	7	88	11	81	18	76	23	73	25	55	44
50 to 64 years	89	10	86	12	85	10	86	12	78	20	71	20	64	32	53	43
65 years and older	85	13	81	15	84	12	83	15	73	20	70	23	63	30	64	33
Region																
East	95	5	84	15	84	11	88	11	79	20	75	23	68	29	64	35
Midwest	92	7	87	12	89	10	89	9	79	17	77	17	68	27	57	41
South	81	19	90	10	86	11	86	13	72	26	66	29	68	29	47	51
West	90	9	90	8	89	7	87	11	79	17	70	26	71	25	52	45
Race																
White	88	11	89	10	88	8	89	10	79	19	73	23	70	27	54	44
Nonwhite	93	7	83	17	79	21	83	17	60	34	62	34	66	28	60	37

Clear Your Record and Own a Gun

Education																
College post graduate	90	9	92	6	91	4	89	8	87	13	76	22	68	30	58	41
Total college[a]	91	9	91	8	92	6	89	10	81	16	77	20	71	26	55	43
No college	87	12	85	14	82	14	85	13	73	24	67	28	67	29	54	44
Politics																
Republican	85	14	86	14	87	11	87	13	77	21	70	29	67	30	48	51
Democrat	94	6	88	12	88	10	91	8	79	18	73	23	70	25	65	34
Independent	87	12	90	8	86	8	84	13	75	22	72	22	68	28	51	46
Income																
$50,000 and over	89	10	91	8	91	6	90	8	84	14	77	20	72	26	52	46
$30,000 to $49,999	92	8	9	19	91	6	86	13	77	21	74	23	67	30	52	47
$20,000 to $29,999	88	12	88	12	87	10	90	9	82	18	76	22	72	23	58	40
Under $20,000	87	11	83	16	79	17	86	12	72	25	66	29	69	28	59	39
Community																
Urban area	93	6	88	11	86	11	89	10	76	20	76	21	72	23	62	35
Suburban area	92	8	89	10	86	9	90	8	83	16	74	24	69	27	56	43
Rural area	79	21	85	13	89	10	82	17	70	28	63	29	64	34	43	55

Note: The "mixed/no opinion" category has been omitted; therefore percents may not sum to 100. For a discussion of public opinion survey sampling procedures, see Appendix 5.

[a] Includes college graduates and persons who attended some college.

Source: George Gallup, Jr., *The Gallup Poll Monthly*, No. 340 (Princeton, NJ: The Gallup Poll, January 1994), pp. 23, 24. Reprinted by permission.

Table 2.65

Respondents favoring selected gun control measures

By demographic characteristics, United States, 1993

Question: "I will read you some proposals for fighting crime. Please say for each if you favor or oppose it. Do you favor or oppose...?"

(Percent reporting they favor the measure)

	Imposing a five-day waiting period between purchase and delivery of a gun	Banning the sale of guns to people under the age of 18	Banning the sale of assault rifles
National	86 %	85 %	69 %
Age			
18 to 24 years	82	80	57
25 to 29 years	85	89	70
30 to 39 years	85	88	65
40 to 49 years	92	90	77
50 to 64 years	85	80	72
65 years and older	84	82	70
Region			
East	87	87	67
Midwest	86	84	69
South	82	83	63
West	89	88	80
Community			
City	86	80	73
Suburban area	88	89	70
Small town	83	82	58
Rural area	77	88	65
Politics			
Republican	83	87	66
Democrat	87	85	71
Independent	89	85	71
Household income			
$50,001 and over	94	92	79
$35,001 to $50,000	91	89	78
$25,001 to $35,000	86	84	68
$15,001 to $25,000	85	85	66
$7,001 to $15,000	78	81	61
$7,000 and under	75	71	63

Note: For a discussion of public opinion survey sampling procedures, see Appendix 5.

Source: Louis Harris, *The Harris Poll* (Los Angeles: Creators Syndicate, Inc., Nov. 24, 1993), pp. 3, 4. Reprinted by permission.

CHAPTER 4
Federal Jurisdictions Firearm Rights Recovery

It is strongly advised, that if you are going to try to get your right to bear arms returned to you on a federal level, for a federal criminal conviction, a copy of your F.B.I. "rap sheet," the most current possible, must be in front of you before you start. It is simple to obtain by writing to the Federal Bureau of Investigation in Washington, D.C. for a copy. You will need a set of fingerprints from your local police or sheriff, proof of identity, and a $17.00 money order made out to the Treasury of the United States. Mail the money, proof of identity, (date of birth, full name, place of birth, Social Security number, etc.), and the fingerprint card, with a written request for your record to:

FBI
Identification Division
Washington, D.C.
20537-9700

Upon receipt of your request, the FBI will pull your record, make you a copy as it currently appears, and mail it back to you. You only need to work on what appears on that record–nothing else. This response of the FBI is through the rules and regulations, Part 16, § 16:32 procedure to obtain an identification record. Remember-the FBI is not responsible for what appears on your record–the agency that sent them the information is responsible–Federal Marshal, DEA, CIA, and the Bureau Office of the FBI, etc., are the ones responsible for whatever is on your "rap sheet". Usually, it is the agency that arrested you. If the record you see is wrong, you can do something about it. And do it before you apply for any post conviction relief. Corrections are not impossible-contact the agency that has reported it wrong or not updated it. In turn, they will contact the FBI for correction. Now, let us say from here that you have obtained a current copy of your FBI record, and that it is right, and you want to restore your right to bear arms.

CRIMES-FIREARMS
Chapter 44-18 § 925
§925. Exceptions: Relief From Disabilities

This federal law, under the above specified caption, allows, of course, for the military to have guns and ammo.
However, it is Section 5. (C) that has influence on your restoration of the right to bear arms. Quoted:
"A person who has been convicted of a crime punishable by imprisonment for a term exceeding one year (a felony) (other than a crime involving the use of a firearm or other weapon or a violation of this chapter or of the National Firearms Act) may make application to the Secretary (Alcohol, Tobacco, & Firearms) for the relief from the disabilities imposed by federal laws with respect to the acquisition, receipt, transfer, shipment, or possession of firearms and incurred by reason of such conviction, and the Secretary (Alcohol, Tobacco, & Firearms) may grant such relief if it is established to his satisfaction that the circumstances regarding the conviction, and the applicant's record and reputation, are such that the applicant will not be likely to act in a manner dangerous to public safety and that the granting of the relief would not be contrary to public interest. A licensed importer, licensed manufacturer, licensed dealer, or licensed collector conducting operations under this chapter (44-USCA-Unites States Code-Annotated), who makes application for relief from disabilities incurred under this chapter by

reason of such a conviction, shall not be barred by such conviction from further operations under his license pending final action on an application for relief filed pursuant to Section (18). Whenever the Secretary grants relief to any person (or dealer or importer) under this section, he shall promptly publish in the *Federal Register* notice of such action, together with the reasons therefore."

(Included in this book are copies of the actual federal statutes for exceptions: Relief from Disabilities, 18 § 925.

For a free application and instructions on filing your motion for Relief From Disability, call Washington, D.C., (202) 927-7777. That is the number for the Bureau of Alcohol, Tobacco and Firearms. It is still suggested that you get a copy of your FBI report before you apply for relief from disability. Please, remember that the conviction you are trying to get relief from disability for must be a federal offense. This law does not work for state convictions. State relief from disability is possible-but not in this format.

Presidential Pardons - Executive Clemency

For purposes of this book, and the convenience of having this information (by scanning and reproducing onto disk) available in hard copy and on 3.5 diskette, the exact forms used by the federal government are presented here. Do not file the instructions pages, but do read the words. Pay particular attention on the part about filing false information-five years in prison and a fine of $250,000.

Before you file, read the entire paperwork. Take note of the five year waiting period, after you have completed all of your sentence, or probation, or parole.

The following forms are to be used in the application of Presidential Pardon which in turn restores all of your civil rights-including the right to bear arms.

Some advice–if you know a federal entity, such as a senator, congressman, federal judge, magistrate, judicial administrator, etc., ask them to give you a recommendation. If you don't know any, try to contact your area's senator and explain to him/her what you are trying to do. Write to them, in Washington, and at their home office. Tell them why you think you deserve a presidential pardon. If they agree, they will help you.

When was the last time you backed a federal political candidate for office with a contribution of your time, efforts or small monetary gift towards the campaign? It wouldn't hurt to find out who your federal representatives are, and when they're up for reelection or election. Let them know you're alive and need their support in your bid for pardon. It can help a lot.

Warning!! Warning!!

In a recent U. S. Supreme Court decision (Beecham V. U. S., May 16, 1994), it was decided that a state pardon does not restore the rights to bear arms if there were federal convictions.

Beecham and Jones were both convicted of felons in possession of firearms, after they had each been convicted in federal courts and several convictions in state courts. State convictions were not considered in the decision. The court held that federal loss of civil rights can only be restored in the federal court of jurisdiction. Both men, Beecham and Jones, had had their civil rights restored to them in their home states, by the state. Simply put, the Supreme Court says that even if you have a full pardon, with restoration of all civil rights, you still do not have the right to bear arms– and the Supreme Court admits that there is no "federal procedure for restoring rights to a federal felon", (with the exception of presidential pardon or executive clemency), but that is O. K., because the states of Arkansas, Indiana, Kentucky, Maryland, Missouri, New Jersey, Oklahoma, Pennsylvania, Rhode Island, Texas, Vermont, and Virginia have no procedure for restoring civil rights to a state felon.

The following pages contain letters and forms that you will become intimately acquainted with in pursuit of a federal pardon.

FedeRAl JuRisdiCTiON FiREARM RiGHTs RECOVERy

U.S. Department of Justice

Pardon Attorney

Washington, D.C. 20530

MAY 27 994

Mr. William Rinehart
300 Spruce Drive, #204
Lafayette, Louisiana 70506

Dear Mr. Rinehart:

    This responds to your letter of April 14, 1994, requesting information on the pardon process.

    We are enclosing forms which you may use in making formal application for pardon. The forms should be carefully and fully completed in accordance with the rules and instructions that are provided. Please note in particular paragraphs two and three of the Information and Instructions on Pardons (the President's clemency powers under the Constitution are limited to federal offenses). The completed forms should be returned to this office for processing and need not be filed in duplicate.

                                Sincerely,

                                Margaret Colgate Love
                                Pardon Attorney

Enclosure

Response to my letter requesting information and forms to apply for a Federal Pardon.

CLEAR YOUR RECORD AND OWN A GUN

U.S. Department of Justice
Office of the Pardon Attorney

OCT 4 1994

Mr. William Rinehart
300 Spruce Drive #204
LaFayette, LA 70506

Request for Pardon Application Form

Enclosed is the form to use in applying for a pardon. The form should be carefully and fully completed in accordance with the rules and instructions that are provided. Please note in particular paragraphs two and three of the Information and Instructions on Pardons. Only federal convictions are subject to presidential pardon and a minimum waiting period of five years after completion of sentence is required before a pardon application may be accepted. See Section 1.2 of the enclosed rules. The completed form should be returned to this office for processing and need not be filed in duplicate.

Federal Jurisdiction Firearm Rights Recovery

RULES GOVERNING PETITIONS FOR EXECUTIVE CLEMENCY

United States Department of Justice

WASHINGTON, D.C.

PART 1 - EXECUTIVE CLEMENCY

Sec.

1.1 Submission of petition; form to be used; contents of petition.
1.2 Eligibility for filing petition for pardon.
1.3 Eligibility for filing petition for commutation of sentence.
1.4 Offenses against the laws of possessions or territories of the United States.
1.5 Disclosure of files.
1.6 Consideration of petitions; recommendations to the President.
1.7 Notification of grant of clemency.
1.8 Notification of denial of clemency.
1.9 Delegation of authority.
1.10 Advisory nature of regulations.

Authority: U.S. Const., Art. II, sec. 2; authority of the President as Chief Executive; and 28 U.S.C. §§ 509, 510.

§ 1.1 Submission of petition; form to be used; contents of petition.

A person seeking executive clemency by pardon, reprieve, commutation of sentence, or remission of fine shall execute a formal petition. The petition shall be addressed to the President of the United States and shall be submitted to the Pardon Attorney, Department of Justice, Washington, D.C. 20530, except for petitions relating to military offenses. Petitions and other required forms may be obtained from the Pardon Attorney. Petition forms for commutation of sentence also may be obtained from the wardens of federal penal institutions. A petitioner applying for executive clemency with respect to military offenses should submit his or her petition directly to the Secretary of the military department that had original jurisdiction over the court-martial trial and conviction of the petitioner. In such a case, a form furnished by the Pardon Attorney may be used but should be modified to meet the needs of the particular case. Each petition for executive clemency should include the information required in the form prescribed by the Attorney General.

§ 1.2 Eligibility for filing petition for pardon.

No petition for pardon should be filed until the expiration of a waiting period of at least five years after the date of the release of the petitioner from confinement or, in case no prison sentence was imposed, until the expiration of a period of at least five years after the date of the conviction of the petitioner. Generally, no petition should be submitted by a person who is on probation, parole, or supervised release.

§ 1.3 Eligibility for filing petition for commutation of sentence.

No petition for commutation of sentence, including remission of fine, should be filed if other forms of judicial or administrative relief are available, except upon a showing of exceptional circumstances.

§ 1.4 Offenses against the laws of possessions or territories of the United States.

Petitions for executive clemency shall relate only to violations of laws of the United States. Petitions relating to violations of laws of the possessions of the United States or territories subject to the jurisdiction of the United States should be submitted to the appropriate official or agency of the possession or territory concerned.

§ 1.5 Disclosure of files.

Petitions, reports, memoranda, and communications submitted or furnished in connection with the consideration of a petition for executive clemency generally shall be available only to the officials concerned with the consideration of the petition. However, they may be made available for inspection, in whole or in part, when in the judgment of the Attorney General their disclosure is required by law or the ends of justice.

§ 1.6 Consideration of petitions; recommendations to the President.

(a) Upon receipt of a petition for executive clemency, the Attorney General shall cause such investigation to be made of the matter as he/she may deem necessary and appropriate, using the services of, or obtaining reports from, appropriate officials and agencies of the Government, including the Federal Bureau of Investigation.

(b) The Attorney General shall review each petition and all pertinent information developed by the investigation and shall determine whether the request for clemency is of sufficient merit to warrant favorable action by the President. The Attorney General shall report in writing his or her recommendation to the President, stating whether in his or her judgment the President should grant or deny the petition.

§ 1.7 Notification of grant of clemency.

When a petition for pardon is granted, the petitioner or his or her attorney shall be notified of such action and the warrant of pardon shall be mailed to the petitioner. When commutation of sentence is granted, the petitioner shall be notified of such action and the warrant of commutation shall be sent to the petitioner through the officer in charge of his or her place of confinement, or directly to the petitioner if he/she is on parole, probation, or supervised release.

§ 1.8 Notification of denial of clemency.

(a) Whenever the President notifies the Attorney General that he has denied a request for clemency, the Attorney General shall so advise the petitioner and close the case.

(b) Except in cases in which a sentence of death has been imposed, whenever the Attorney General recommends that the President deny a request for clemency and the President does not disapprove or take other action with respect to that adverse recommendation within 30 days after the date of its submission to him, it shall be presumed that the President concurs in that adverse recommendation of the Attorney General, and the Attorney General shall so advise the petitioner and close the case.

§ 1.9 Delegation of authority.

The Attorney General may delegate to any officer of the Department of Justice any of his or her duties or responsibilities under §§ 1.1 through 1.8.

§ 1.10 Advisory nature of regulations.

The regulations contained in this part are advisory only and for the internal guidance of Department of Justice personnel. They create no enforceable rights in persons applying for executive clemency, nor do they restrict the authority granted to the President under Article II, Section 2 of the Constitution.

Dated: August 23, 1993.
Janet Reno,
Attorney General.

Dated: October 12, 1993.
Approved:
William J. Clinton,
President.

Published in the FEDERAL REGISTER of the National Archives of the United States, October 18, 1993 Vol. 58, No. 199, at pages 53658 and 53659.

CLEAR YOUR RECORD AND OWN A GUN

INFORMATION AND INSTRUCTIONS ON PARDONS
Please read carefully before completing the pardon application

1. Submit the petition to the Office of the Pardon Attorney

All petitions, except petitions relating to military offenses (see paragraph 6 below), should be forwarded to the Pardon Attorney, Department of Justice, 500 First Street N.W., 4th Floor, Washington, D.C. 20530. It is important that the completed pardon petition be entirely legible; therefore, please print or type. *The form must be completed fully and accurately in order to be considered.* You may attach to the petition additional pages and documents which amplify or clarify your answer to any question.

2. Federal convictions only

Only *federal* convictions are subject to presidential pardon since the federal pardon power does not extend to state offenses. Necessary information concerning the conviction may be obtained from the clerk of the federal court where you were convicted.

3. Five-year waiting period required

A minimum waiting period of five years after completion of sentence is required before anyone who has been convicted of violating a federal law is eligible to apply for a presidential pardon. The eligibility waiting period required by the Rules Governing Petitions for Executive Clemency (as published in Title 28, Code of Federal Regulations, §1.1 et seq.) begins on the date of the petitioner's release from confinement. If the conviction resulted in probation or a fine and no term of imprisonment, the waiting period begins on the date of conviction. In addition, the petitioner should have satisfied the penalty imposed, including all probation, parole, or supervised release. The waiting period is designed to afford the petitioner a reasonable time in which to demonstrate an ability to lead a responsible, productive and law-abiding life to the betterment of the community. Accordingly, offenses committed subsequent to the offense for which pardon is sought may lengthen the minimum eligibility period for pardons. Waiver of any portion of the waiting period is rarely granted and then only in the most exceptional circumstances.

4. Reason for seeking pardon

In answering question 15 on page 6 of the petition, you should state the specific purpose for which you are seeking pardon and attach documentary evidence (e.g., copies of applicable provisions of state constitutions, statutes or regulations and/or letters from appropriate officials of administrative agencies, professional associations, licensing authorities or the like) that a pardon will be helpful to you in accomplishing the purpose for which it is sought. Most disabilities attendant upon a federal felony conviction, e.g., the right to vote and hold public office, are imposed by state rather than federal law, and may be removed by state action. The federal pardon process is exacting and may be more time-consuming than state procedures for restoration of civil rights, and you may therefore wish to consult in this regard with the Governor or other appropriate authorities of the state of your residence (e.g., the state board of pardons and paroles).

5. Multiple federal convictions

If you are seeking pardon of more than one federal conviction, the most recent conviction should be shown in response to question 2 of the petition and the form completed as to that conviction. The information requested in questions 2 through 5 of the petition concerning any other federal convictions, including convictions by military courts-martial, should be provided on an attachment. Any federal charges not resulting in conviction should be reported in the space provided for prior and subsequent arrests (question 10).

6. Pardon of a military offense

If you are requesting pardon of a military offense only, you should submit your completed petition directly to the Secretary of the military department which had original jurisdiction in your case, completing questions 2 through 5 and question 12 of the petition form to show all pertinent information concerning your court-martial trial and conviction. You should be aware that pardon of a military offense will not change the character of a military discharge. This may be accomplished only by appropriate military authorities.

*United States Department of Justice
Office of the Pardon Attorney
Washington, D.C. 20530*

September 1994

Federal Jurisdiction Firearm Rights Recovery

7. Additional arrest record
You must disclose in answering question 10 *any* additional arrest record (civilian or military), whether local, state or foreign, both prior and subsequent to the offense for which you are seeking pardon. Your answer should list every violation, including traffic violations that resulted in an arrest or criminal charge. Your failure to disclose any such arrest, whether or not it resulted in conviction, may be construed as falsification of the petition.

8. Credit status and civil lawsuits
In response to question 11, you must list all delinquent credit obligations, whether or not you dispute them. You must also list all civil lawsuits in which you were named as a party, whether as plaintiff or defendant. You must also list all unpaid tax obligations, whether federal, state or local. You may submit explanatory material in connection with any of these matters, e.g., an agreed method of payment for indebtedness.

9. Character references
At least three character affidavits must accompany the petition. If you submit more than three, you should designate the three persons whom you consider to be primary references. The affidavit forms provided are preferred; however, letters of recommendation which evidence therein a knowledge of the offense for which you seek pardon may be substituted. Persons submitting references should not be related to you by blood or marriage.

10. Effect of a pardon
A presidential pardon will *not* erase or expunge your record of conviction. A presidential pardon is a sign of forgiveness and not of vindication. It does not connote or establish innocence. Therefore, you will still be required to report the conviction where such information is required. In addition, in considering the merits of a pardon petition, pardon officials take into account statements by the petitioner relating to acceptance of responsibility, remorse and atonement.

11. Scope of investigation
Pardon officials conduct a very thorough review in determining a petitioner's worthiness for relief. Petitioners should therefore be prepared for a detailed inquiry into their background and current activities. Among the factors entering into this determination are the nature, seriousness, and recentness of the offense, petitioner's prior and/or subsequent criminal record, any specific hardship the petitioner may be suffering by reason of the conviction (see paragraph 4 above), and the nature and extent of an applicant's post-conviction involvement in community service, charitable or other meritorious activities. Regarding the latter, submission of information concerning the petitioner's noteworthy community contributions is encouraged.

12. Presidential pardon authority
The power to grant pardons is vested in the President alone. No hearing is held and there is no appeal from an adverse decision in a pardon matter. The specific reasons for the action taken in a pardon matter are not disclosed. If your petition is denied, you may submit a new petition for consideration two years from the date of denial if new and significant information or substantially changed circumstances support favorable action.

For more information, you may contact the *Office of the Pardon Attorney* at the address provided in paragraph 1 above or by telephone at (202) 616-6070.

CLEAR YOUR RECORD AND OWN A GUN

IMPORTANT NOTICE
To Applicants for Pardon

The following notice is provided pursuant to the Privacy Act of 1974 and may help you to understand what is involved in petitioning for pardon and why we need to obtain certain information about you.

The information which we request from you on the accompanying pardon application form, and in the event you are interviewed by an agent of the United States Government, is needed to help provide the basis of an informed judgment as to whether or not you should be granted a pardon. This is our only purpose in asking you to complete and sign the application and, if necessary, requesting that an investigation be made into your character and activities. You are under no obligation to furnish any information. However, unless you do provide us with all the information requested, we may be unable to process your application. Failure to provide your Social Security number will not prejudice your case.

In making inquiries with respect to these matters, an agent of the United States Government may interview you, as well as persons who have executed character affidavits or have written letters of reference on your behalf, neighbors, former and present employers, associates and other individuals who may be able to provide relevant information concerning you. While such inquiries are made discreetly and a reasonable effort is made not to disclose the underlying nature of the investigation, we cannot assure that the reason for the inquiry will not become known to some or all of the persons interviewed.

Our authority for requesting this information is the United States Constitution, Article II, Section 2 (the pardon clause); Order No. 1798-93, 58 Fed. Reg. 53658 and 53659 (1993), codified in 28 C.F.R. §§ 1.1 et seq. (the rules governing petitions for executive clemency); and Order of the Attorney General No. 1012-83, 48 Fed. Reg. 22290 (1983), as codified in 28 C.F.R. §§ 0.35 and 0.36 (the authority of the Pardon Attorney).

Executive clemency files are compiled and maintained to provide for the exercise of the President's constitutional pardon power and are routinely made available to him, members of his staff and other officials concerned with clemency proceedings. After the President has taken final action on an application, a public notice is prepared describing each grant of clemency (and may be prepared for each denial in cases of substantial public interest). A copy of each warrant of clemency is maintained in the Office of the Pardon Attorney as a public and official record.

Upon specific request, we advise anyone who asks whether a named person has been granted or denied clemency. Disclosure of the contents of executive clemency files to anyone may be made by the Pardon Attorney when the disclosure is required by law or the ends of justice. In addition, the pendency of an application is confirmed upon request, unless extraordinary considerations of privacy are presented in a particular case that outweigh the public interest in having access to this information. If you believe such privacy considerations are present in your case, you should so inform us in writing when you submit the application.

United States Department of Justice
Office of the Pardon Attorney
Washington, D.C. 20530

September 1994

Federal Jurisdiction Firearm Rights Recovery

Petition for Pardon After Completion of Sentence

Please read accompanying instructions carefully before beginning. Typewrite or print the answers in ink. Each question must be answered fully, truthfully, and accurately. If the space for any answer is insufficient, petitioner may complete answer on a separate sheet of paper and attach it to the petition. Submission of material, false information is punishable by imprisonment of up to five years and a fine of not more than $250,000. 18 U.S.C. §§ 1001 and 3571.

To The President Of The United States:

The undersigned petitioner prays for a pardon and in support thereof states as follows:

1. Full name:_____
                 First   *Middle*   *Last*

   Address:_____
          Number *Street*   *City*   *State*   *Zip Code*

   Telephone Number (include area code):_____

   Social Security No._____. Date and place of birth:_____

   Are you a United States citizen? ❏ yes ❏ no. If not, state nationality and give alien registration

   number:_____. If naturalized U.S. citizen, furnish date and

   place of naturalization:_____

   State in full every other name by which you have been known, including name under which you were convicted, the reason for the use of another name, and the dates during which you were so known. If married woman, give maiden name (if different).

   _____

Offense(s) For Which Pardon Is Sought

2. Petitioner was convicted on a plea of _____ in the United States District Court
                                   guilty, not guilty, nolo contendere

   for the _____ District of _____ of the crime of:

   _____
   (Describe specific offense)

   _____

   and was sentenced on _____, 19___ to ❏ imprisonment ❏ probation for _____
                                                                (length of sentence)

   and/or to pay a fine of $_____. Restitution in the amount of $_____

   ❏ has ❏ has not been made. Petitioner was ____ years of age when the offense was committed.

3. Petitioner began service of the sentence of ❏ imprisonment ❏ probation on _____, 19___;

   was released on _____, 19___ from _____; and was finally
                                            (Federal Institution)

   discharged by expiration of sentence on _____, 19___. If the fine, restitution,

   assessments or costs were not paid in full, explain why:

   _____

United States Department of Justice
Office of the Pardon Attorney
Washington, D.C. 20530

September 1994

Clear Your Record and Own a Gun

4. Give a complete and detailed account of offense, including dates (or time span) of offense, names of codefendants and, when applicable, amount of money involved. You are expected to describe factual basis of your offense completely and accurately and not rely on criminal code citations or name references only. If your conviction resulted from plea agreement, you should describe fully the extent of your total involvement in the criminal transaction(s), in addition to charge(s) to which you pled guilty. (Attach separate sheet if necessary.)

_____

_____

_____

_____

_____

_____

_____

_____

_____

5. Petitioner ❑ did ❑ did not appeal the conviction.
   If appealed, please provide date of decision(s) by Court of Appeals and, if applicable, the Supreme Court. Please also provide citations to any published judicial opinion(s) or a copy of unpublished opinion(s).

Biographical Information

6. Current marital status: ❑ Single ❑ Married ❑ Divorced ❑ Widowed ❑ Separated
   For each marriage give the following: name of spouse, date and place of spouse's birth, date and place of marriage, and, if applicable, date and place of divorce:

name of spouse	date/place of birth
date/place of marriage	date/place of divorce
name of spouse	date/place of birth
date/place of marriage	date/place of divorce
name of spouse	date/place of birth
date/place of marriage	date/place of divorce

7. List your children by name, and furnish date and place of birth for each:
   If you do not have custody of any minor children, indicate whether you pay child support.)

name of child	date/place of birth
name of child	date/place of birth
name of child	date/place of birth
name of child	date/place of birth
name of child	date/place of birth

FEDERAL JURISDICTION FIREARM RIGHTS RECOVERY

Residences

8. List every place you have lived since the conviction, beginning with the present. (An optional continuation page is provided for your convenience.)

Date you moved to present address (month/year):	Number and Street		
	City	State	Zip Code

From (month/year):	Number and Street		
To (month/year):	City	State	Zip Code

From (month/year):	Number and Street		
To (month/year):	City	State	Zip Code

From (month/year):	Number and Street		
To (month/year):	City	State	Zip Code

Employment History

9. List all periods of employment and unemployment since the conviction. Indicate means of support during any periods of unemployment. (An optional continuation page is provided for your convenience.)

Present employer		Telephone (include area code)	
Date you began this employment (month/year):	Number and Street		
	City	State	Zip Code
Type of business		Position	

Employer		Telephone (include area code)	
Began (month/year):	Number and Street		
Ended (month/year):	City	State	Zip Code
Type of business		Position	

Employer		Telephone (include area code)	
Began (month/year):	Number and Street		
Ended (month/year):	City	State	Zip Code
Type of business		Position	

Have you ever been discharged from employment for any reason? ❑ yes ❑ no.

Have you ever resigned after being informed that your employer intended to discharge you for any reason? ❑ yes ❑ no.

If you answered yes to either question, explain fully below:

_____
_____

Clear Your Record and Own a Gun

Petition for Pardon After Completion of Sentence

Residences

From (month/year):	Number and Street		
To (month/year):	City	State	Zip Code

From (month/year):	Number and Street		
To (month/year):	City	State	Zip Code

From (month/year):	Number and Street		
To (month/year):	City	State	Zip Code

From (month/year):	Number and Street		
To (month/year):	City	State	Zip Code

Employment History

Employer		Telephone (include area code)	
Began (month/year):	Number and Street		
Ended (month/year):	City	State	Zip Code
Type of business		Position	

Employer		Telephone (include area code)	
Began (month/year):	Number and Street		
Ended (month/year):	City	State	Zip Code
Type of business		Position	

Employer		Telephone (include area code)	
Began (month/year):	Number and Street		
Ended (month/year):	City	State	Zip Code
Type of business		Position	

Employer		Telephone (include area code)	
Began (month/year):	Number and Street		
Ended (month/year):	City	State	Zip Code
Type of business		Position	

Federal Jurisdiction Firearm Rights Recovery

Prior and Subsequent Criminal Record

10. Have you ever been arrested, taken into custody, held for investigation or questioning, or charged by any law enforcement authority, whether federal, state, local or foreign, either as a juvenile or adult? ❑ yes ❑ no.

    For each incident list date, nature of offense charged, factual circumstances, law enforcement authority involved, location and disposition. You must list every violation, including traffic violations that resulted in an arrest or criminal charge; for example, driving under the influence. (Any omission will be considered a falsification.)

    _____
    _____
    _____
    _____
    _____
    _____
    _____
    _____
    _____
    _____
    _____
    _____

Civil and Financial Information

11. Are you in default or delinquent in any way in the performance or discharge of any debt or obligation imposed upon you? ❑ yes ❑ no.

    Since the conviction, have any liens (including federal or state tax liens) or any lawsuits been filed against you, or have you been a party to a bankruptcy proceeding? ❑ yes ❑ no.

    Do you have pending any judicial or administrative proceedings with the federal or state governments? ❑ yes ❑ no.

    If you answered yes to any question, explain fully below:

    _____
    _____
    _____
    _____
    _____
    _____
    _____
    _____
    _____

Clear Your Record and Own a Gun

Military Record

12. Have you ever served in the armed forces of the United States? ❏ yes ❏ no.

    If yes, indicate the nature of the discharge(s) _____

    If other than honorable, specify type and circumstances surrounding your release(s):

    _____

    _____

    _____

    List the dates of service: _____

    Serial number(s): _____ Branch(es) of service: _____

    List decorations, if any: _____

    While serving in the armed forces, were you the recipient of non-judicial punishment, or the defendant in any court-martial? ❏ yes ❏ no.

    If yes, state fully the nature of the charge, relevant facts, disposition of the proceedings, the date thereof, and the name and address of the authority in possession of the records thereof. (If you were convicted of an offense by court-martial, provide on an attachment the same information with respect to each conviction that is required in questions 2 through 5.)

    _____

    _____

    _____

    _____

Civil Rights Restoration.

13. Have you received restoration of your civil rights (for example, a state pardon, a certification of restoration of civil rights, or a certificate of discharge)? ❏ yes ❏ no.

    If yes, indicate date of restoration and attach copy of the document(s) evidencing the state's action.

    _____

14. Have you applied for <u>removal of your federal firearms disabilities</u>? ❏ yes ❏ no. (Through ATF)

    If yes, was your application granted? ❏ yes ❏ no.

    Have you applied for removal of your state firearms disabilities? ❏ yes ❏ no.

    If yes, was your application granted? ❏ yes ❏ no.

    Please provide date(s) of determination(s). If your firearms privileges have been restored, attach a copy of the document evidencing the agency's action.

    _____

Federal Jurisdiction Firearm Rights Recovery

Reasons for Seeking Pardon

15. State your reasons for seeking a pardon. Please refer to paragraphs 4 and 11 in the attached Information and Instructions on Pardons. (As pointed out in paragraph 10 of the attached instructions, a pardon is a sign of forgiveness. Accordingly, in the usual request for pardon you should not reargue your case, assert innocence, or otherwise attack the validity of your conviction.)

_____
_____
_____
_____
_____
_____
_____
_____
_____
_____
_____
_____

Certification and Personal Oath

I hereby certify that all answers to the above questions and all statements contained herein are true, and I understand that any misstatements of material facts contained in this petition may cause adverse action on my petition for pardon, in addition to subjecting me to any other penalties provided by law.

In petitioning the President of the United States for pardon, I do solemnly swear that I will be law-abiding and will support and defend the Constitution of the United States against all enemies, foreign and domestic, and that I take this obligation freely and without any mental reservation whatsoever, So Help Me God.

Respectfully submitted this _____ day of _____, 19_____.

_____
(signature of petitioner)

Subscribed and sworn to before me this _____ day of _____, 19_____.

_____
Notary Public

Clear Your Record and Own a Gun

United States Department of Justice
Office of the Pardon Attorney
Washington, D.C. 20530

Character Affidavit
on behalf of

_____
(print or type name of petitioner)

In support of the application of the above named petitioner to the President of the United States for pardon, I, _____,
(print or type name of affiant)

residing at _____,
Number   Street   City   State   Zip Code

whose occupation is _____,

certify that I have personally known the petitioner for _____ years. Except as otherwise indicated below, petitioner has behaved since the conviction in a moral and law-abiding manner. My knowledge of petitioner's reputation, conduct and activities, including whether the petitioner has been arrested or had any other trouble with public authorities and has been steadily employed, is as follows:

_____
_____
_____
_____
_____
_____
_____
_____
_____
_____

I do solemnly swear that the foregoing information is true and correct to the best of my knowledge and belief.

_____
(signature of affiant)

Subscribed and sworn to before me this _____ day of _____, 19____.

_____
Notary Public

Federal Jurisdiction Firearm Rights Recovery

United States Department of Justice
Office of the Pardon Attorney
Washington, D.C. 20530

Character Affidavit
on behalf of

_____
(print or type name of petitioner)

In support of the application of the above named petitioner to the President of the United States for pardon, I, _____,
(print or type name of affiant)

residing at _____ _____ _____ _____ _____,
Number Street   City   State   Zip Code

whose occupation is _____,

certify that I have personally known the petitioner for _____ years. Except as otherwise indicated below, petitioner has behaved since the conviction in a moral and law-abiding manner. My knowledge of petitioner's reputation, conduct and activities, including whether the petitioner has been arrested or had any other trouble with public authorities and has been steadily employed, is as follows:

_____
_____
_____
_____
_____
_____
_____
_____
_____

I do solemnly swear that the foregoing information is true and correct to the best of my knowledge and belief.

_____
(signature of affiant)

Subscribed and sworn to before me this _____ day of _____, 19____.

_____
Notary Public

CLEAR YOUR RECORD AND OWN A GUN

United States Department of Justice
Office of the Pardon Attorney
Washington, D.C. 20530

CHARACTER AFFIDAVIT
on behalf of

_____
(print or type name of petitioner)

In support of the application of the above named petitioner to the President of the United States for pardon, I, _____,
(print or type name of affiant)

residing at _____,
   Number   Street   City   State   Zip Code

whose occupation is _____,

certify that I have personally known the petitioner for _____ years. Except as otherwise indicated below, petitioner has behaved since the conviction in a moral and law-abiding manner. My knowledge of petitioner's reputation, conduct and activities, including whether the petitioner has been arrested or had any other trouble with public authorities and has been steadily employed, is as follows:

_____

_____

_____

_____

_____

_____

_____

_____

_____

I do solemnly swear that the foregoing information is true and correct to the best of my knowledge and belief.

_____
(signature of affiant)

Subscribed and sworn to before me this _____ day of _____, 19____.

_____
Notary Public

FEDERAL JURISDICTION FIREARM RIGHTS RECOVERY

AUTHORIZATION FOR RELEASE OF INFORMATION

> Carefully read this authorization to release information about you, then sign and date it in ink.

I authorize any investigator, special agent, or other duly accredited representative of the Federal Bureau of Investigation, the Department of Defense, and any authorized Federal agency, to obtain any information relating to my activities from schools, residential management agents, employers, criminal justice agencies, retail business establishments, or other sources of information. This information may include, but is not limited to, my academic, residential, achievement, performance, attendance, disciplinary, employment history, and criminal history record information.

I understand that, for financial or lending institutions, medical institutions, hospitals, health care professionals, and other sources of information, a separate specific release will or may be needed, and I may be contacted for such a release at a later date.

I further authorize the Federal Bureau of Investigation, the Department of Defense, and any other authorized agency, to request criminal record information about me from criminal justice agencies for the purpose of determining my suitability for executive clemency.

I authorize custodians of records and sources of information pertaining to me to release such information upon request of the investigator, special agent, or other duly accredited representative of any Federal agency authorized above regardless of any previous agreement to the contrary.

I understand that the information released by records custodians and sources of information is for official use by the Federal Government only for the purposes provided in connection with the processing of this clemency application and may be redisclosed by the Government only as authorized by law.

Copies of this authorization that show my signature are as valid as the original release signed by me. This authorization is valid for two (2) years from the date signed.

Signature (sign in ink)		
Full Name (type or print legibly)		Date Signed
Other Names Used		
Street Address		
City	State	ZIP Code
Home Telephone Number (include area code)	Social Security Number	

United States Deparatment of Justice
Office of the Pardon Attorney
Washington, D.C. 20530

September 1994

Chapter 5
California Firearm Rights Recovery

Just as the federal penal system has its own way of applying for pardon/clemency, and granting the restoration of the right to bear arms, so does California. As stated, in the federal system, you have two ways to restore your rights-by direct application to the Secretary, Bureau of Alcohol, Tobacco & Firearms, and applying directly to the President of the United States for a full pardon for a federal crime. California has a method that recognizes rehabilitation through the court first, then the court recommends your pardon to the state governor for you. It is under Title 6, Reprieves-Pardons-Commutation, Chapter 3.5, page 693 of the California Penal Code, 1994 Compact Edition. As with the federal system, this law deals only with felony convictions. (Misdemeanor convictions will come later-however, misdemeanor convictions do not revoke your right to bear arms, nor take away your civil rights.)

For the purposes of this book, some of the more ambiguous and non-pertinent laws have been deleted in the hope that the reader will not get too bogged down in the paperwork. To put it clearly, in California– as opposed to most other states where you would apply to the state pardon board, and they would in turn make a recommendation to the governor– California requires that you take your case back to court first, in order to prove your worthiness and rehabilitative efforts-and then the court makes the recommendation directly to the governor. Myself, I applaud that method–it leaves no doubt who is ready to get back on the right track. Here is the exact procedure, as it appears in the California Penal Code:

It is strongly advised that you read this very carefully, more than once, before you do anything. Make sure that all the steps and rules that are demanded of you can be complied with before you start-particularly the waiting periods, and the proof of rehabilitation.

REPRIEVES, PARDONS, and COMMUTATIONS
Chapter 3.5, Title 6, Procedure for Restoration of Rights and Application for Pardon.

Penal Code Sections 4852.01-4852.21.

§4582.01. Petition for Certificate of Rehabilitation & Pardon; application of Chapter:

(a) Any person convicted of a felony who has been released from a state prison or other state penal institution or agency in California, whether discharged on completion of the term for which he was sentenced or released on parole prior to May 13, 1943, who has not been incarcerated in a state prison or other state penal institution or agency since his release and who presents satisfactory evidence of a three-year residency in this state immediately prior to the filing of an application for Certificate of Rehabilitation & Pardon provided for by this chapter may file such a petition pursuant to this chapter.

(That means that if you were arrested and convicted before May 13, 1943, you would use this law to apply for a Pardon. However, if you did apply under those circumstances, and you were at least eighteen years old before you went to prison, you would now be at least seventy years old, something the court might consider).

(b) Any person convicted of a felony who, on May 13, 1943, was confined in a state prison or other institution or agency to which he was committed and any person convicted of a felony after that date who is committed to a state prison or other penal institution may file a petition for Certificate of Rehabilitation pursuant to the provisions of this chapter.

(The difference in a. & b. are simple-in a., you apply for a pardon-in b., you can apply for clemency (reduction of sentence) or pardon while still incarcerated. Either way, and in any case, for a Governor's Pardon, you follow these rules.)

(c) Any person convicted of a felony (of which) the accusatory pleading (charges) of which has been dismissed pursuant to Section 1203.4 (Misdemeanor charges changed from nolo contendre– "no contest" or guilty, to charges dismissed and given relief from disability of record) may file for a certificate of rehabilitation and pardon pursuant to the provisions of this chapter; provided the petitioner, (you) have not been incarcerated in any prison, jail, detention facility, or other penal institution or agency since the dismissal (of the charges) and is not on probation for the commission of any other felony, and petitioner presents satisfactory evidence (rent receipts, utilities receipts, pay check stubs, etc), of residence in California, prior to the filing of the petition. (Explained more fully under "misdemeanor section").

Now, the question arises how long you must wait until you can apply to the court for the Certificate of Rehabilitation, and get the pardon, and restore the right to bear arms? Not all sentences carry the same amount of 'waiting time'.

§4852.03 Period of Rehabilitation; Determination of Period.

(a) The period of rehabilitation shall begin to run upon the discharge (release from prison or jail), from custody due to his/her completion of term of sentence, or release on probation or parole, whichever is sooner. (The rehabilitation time is running while you are on probation or parole-you don't wait until it's over to file). The period of time of rehabilitation shall constitute a period of three years residence in this state, plus a period of time determined by the following rules:

1. To the three years shall be added four years (a total of seven years) for the following crimes: death of a fetus, kidnapping for ransom, assault-while in prison doing life with the

means to great bodily harm, (a weapon), or causing death by explosive devices, or any other sentence that carries a life sentence.

2. To the three years residency, shall be added two years (totaling five years), for any offense which is not listed in paragraph 1., and does not carry a life sentence.

3. The trial court hearing the application for (your) the application of Certificate of Rehabilitation may, if the defendant (you) was ordered to serve consecutive (back-to-back) sentences, order that his/her statutory period of rehabilitation be extended-which when combined will not be more than all the sentences added together.

4. Any person released from custody before May 13, 1943 is not subject to these Rules.

(b) Unless, and until the (time) period of rehabilitation has passed, the petitioner (you) shall be ineligible to file for a Certificate of Rehabilitation (and, the right to bear arms.)

(c) A change of residence within the state does not interrupt the time period of rehabilitation. (You can move anywhere within the state of California-the time goes on.)

§4852.04

You can hire a lawyer, if you want, but the State of California will furnish one for you for free. If you're under thirty, you can also get help from the California Youth Authority, for free.

You know that your conduct during your rehabilitation period has to be free from any arrest, or trouble from the law, and you have to exhibit good moral character. You must obey the laws of the land. Keep your nose clean.

WHERE TO FILE THE APPLICATION FOR CERTIFICATE OF REHABILITATION:

If you have met all the criteria, i.e., the waiting period, a clean record, no arrests, etc., then you are ready to file.

Your application, (a blank application is available at any County Clerk of Court office), in the California Superior Court where you live. The filing is free. Remember, you must have been in California for at least three years, continuously, prior to filing.

NOTIFICATION OF FILING
§4852.07
Petition; notice of filing, officials to whom given; notice of time hearing, time for service.

The petitioner, (you) shall give notice of the filing of the petition (for Certificate of Rehabilitation) to the district attorney of the county in which it is filed, to the district attorney in which the offense occurred, (if not the same one), and each county in which the petitioner was convicted of a felony or of a crime where the case was dismissed and to the office of the governor of California, together with a notice of the time of the hearing, at least thirty days before the hearing.

Remember, an attorney can be furnished to you at no cost, as well as help from the county probation/parole office, and the Youth Authority if you're under thirty. If you want any of these people to help you, ask the judge where you file to assign you a lawyer. Remember that you can get a blank application for Certificate of Rehabilitation from any county clerk of court. They are free, and come with instructions.

CERTIFICATE OF REHABILITATION
(This is what you're after)

§4852.13
"If, at the hearing, the court finds that the petitioner has demonstrated by his course of conduct and his rehabilitation and fitness to exercise all of the civil and political rights of citizenship, the court shall make an order declaring that the petitioner has been rehabilitated, and recommending that the governor grant a full pardon."

PARDON
§4852.16
"The certified copy of the Certificate of Rehabilitation shall constitute an application for a full pardon (which the governor can grant without any further action).

REMEDY

§4852.19
"This chapter shall be construed as a procedure for the restoration of rights and an application for pardon"

EFFECTS OF FULL PARDON

CHAPTER 4

§4853
"—to restore to the convicted person all rights, privileges, – –lost to him by reason of that conviction (including the right to bear arms.)

FIREARMS

§4854
"In the granting of a pardon to a person, the governor may provide that the person is entitled to exercise the right to own, possess, and keep any type of firearm that may be lawfully owned by other citizens."

SUMMARY ON CALIFORNIA FELONIES

Using the above California statutes on Application for Certificate of Rehabilitation, together with the required waiting period required by the court, you can get your right to bear arms back, in spite of a felony conviction. Remember, it costs you nothing for help in California-the assignment of an attorney is free, the help from Probation/Parole is free, and if you're under thirty years old, the help from the Youth Authority is free.

To obtain an application for Certificate of Rehabilitation or ask questions of the process, call the governor, at (916) 445-2841, and ask for the legal department. For personal questions, dial the number and then press "3" on a touch tone phone.

MISDEMEANORS IN CALIFORNIA

ON THE SEALING OF RECORDS

Definition of a "Misdemeanor" in California:
"Except in cases where a different punishment is prescribed by any law of this state, every offense declared to be a misdemeanor (less serious than a felony) is punishable by imprisonment in the county jail, (as opposed to a prison) not exceeding six (6) months, or by fine not exceeding one thousand ($1000) dollars, or by both." [In most states, a good rule of thumb to know a misdemeanor from a felony is whether or not the sentence was or could have been over a year in prison or jail. If it was or could have been over a year, it was a felony.]

THE SEALING OF COURT RECORDS

Another way to get your right to bear arms restored is to get your record sealed, as if an arrest never happened. In California, there are several ways to do this. However, bear in mind that a misdemeanor does not prevent you from having a weapon, in most cases.

FOR PERSONS ARRESTED WHEN A MINOR

§ 851.7 (Synopsis)
(a) Any person who has been arrested for a misdemeanor, with or without warrant, while a minor, may, during or after minority (after turning twenty-one years old) petition (ask by motion) the court in which the proceedings occurred or, if there were no court proceedings, the court in whose jurisdiction the arrest occurred, for an order sealing the records in the case, including any record of arrest—if, charges were dropped, the officer did not arrest, or he was acquitted.
(b)—the case shall be deemed not to have occurred.

SEALING AND DESTRUCTION OF RECORDS

§851.8
In any case where an arrest has occurred but no Accusatory Pleading, has been filed (no charges were filed), the person may petition the law enforcement agency (as opposed to the court, and even if you are an adult) to destroy its record.

MISDEMEANOR SENTENCE SERVED
DISMISSAL OF CHARGE
RELEASE FROM PENALTIES & DISABILITIES

§1203.4a
(a) Every defendant (you) convicted of a misdemeanor and not granted Probation shall, at any time after the lapse of one (1) year from the date of the pronouncement, if he/she has complied with and performed the sentence of the court, is not then serving a sentence for any offense, (and is not charged with any offense), and has, since being sentenced lived an honest and upright life, and obeyed the laws of the land, (simply put, caught no more cases) be permitted to withdraw his plea of guilty or no contest and plead not guilty and the court shall thereupon dismiss (the charges), or if he or she has been convicted after a plea of not guilty, the court shall set aside the verdict of guilty; and in either case the court shall thereupon dismiss the (charges), against such defendant, who shall thereafter be released from all penalties and disabilities resulting from that conviction.

(On misdemeanors, whether you pled guilty, or no contest, or went to trial and were found guilty by a judge or jury, at the end of a year after the sentence you can apply to get the charges dropped. That also restores all rights you may have lost.) [Narcotics convictions are covered under section 12021. Traffic convictions are not covered by this statute, meaning they can still revoke your license.]

Certain Misdemeanor Convictions
Sealing of Records

§1203.45
(This law has a direct bearing on the above statute- in regards to additional relief if a minor).

(a) In any case in which a person was under the age of eighteen at the time of a misdemeanor, and has already received relief or is eligible for relief under 1203.4a— the person can petition the court to seal the record— . Thereafter, the arrest, conviction, or other proceeding shall be deemed as to not have happened (Sealing does not erase the record, but it can only be used in the event of the commission of another crime for investigation purposes).

NARCOTICS CONVICTIONS/ADDICTIONS: PEACE OFFICER RELIEF FROM CONVICTION AUTHORIZATION TO HAVE WEAPONS

§12021.
(2) Any person—employed as a peace Officer— whose employment or livelihood is dependent on the ability to legally possess a firearm, who is subject to the prohibition imposed by this subdivision because of a conviction--may petition the court only once for relief from this prohibition.

(Must be filed in the same court as the conviction, with the same judge) You cannot have a previous conviction. If the court finds there is no other prohibition, the petitioner is likely to use a firearm in a safe and lawful manner, —the court will require the petitioner to participate in counseling as deemed appropriate by the court—the court may reduce or eliminate the prohibition— or otherwise grant relief. (For more information on law enforcement officers and availability for use of this statute, see penal code).

Certainly, there are bound to be more ways to restore the right to bear arms in California, and it is advisable that if one cannot be found among the methods within this book, it doesn't mean that way doesn't exist. The problem with this kind of law is, no one advertises it. You sometimes have to go looking for it. Any sizable library has a copy of the penal and civil code. All law libraries have them. One can be bought for twenty-six dollars at any book store that sells law books. The easiest way to file any motion with any court–if you don't want to use a lawyer– is to ask the Clerk at that court for a sample of an old motion. Copy it, take it home and use it to make your own. There are so many sources of information available to anyone who wants to regain their rights –legal aide, indigent defendant attorneys, law school third year students, law libraries, and this book.

I do not propose to be an attorney, but I can use my own experiences, as I have throughout this book. Good luck and God bless.

TELEPHONE NUMBERS

California Dept. of Justice (916) 227-3812
California Dept. of Comm. Relations (916) 445-1114
California Dept. of Legal Affairs (916) 445-0873
Governor Pete Wilson's Office (916) 445-2841
California Bar Assoc. (415) 561-8200
McGeorge Law School (916) 739-7161
UNC Law School (916) 447-7223
America's Book Store (Ships law books) (916) 441-0410

The following pages contain copies from the Governor's office of information on how to apply for a pardon and Certificate of Rehabilitation.

California Firearms Rights Recovery

HOW TO APPLY FOR A PARDON

State of California
Office of the Governor
State Capitol
Sacramento, CA 95814

Statement of Philosophy

A Governor's pardon restores certain citizenship rights to the individual who has demonstrated a high standard of constructive behavior following conviction for an offense. A pardon shall not be issued unless it has been earned. Obtaining a pardon is a distinct achievement based upon proof of a useful, productive and law-abiding life following conviction. It is a worthy and admirable goal, requiring sincere effort and commitment.

In accord with the above philosophy, pardon applications will not be considered unless an applicant has been discharged from probation or parole for at least ten years and has not engaged in further criminal activity during that period. While the receipt of a Certificate of Rehabilitation will be considered in evaluating a pardon application, it is but one factor and is not the sole determinant. The ten-year rule may be waived in truly exceptional circumstances if the applicant can demonstrate an earlier, specific need for the pardon.

Once the above-discussed criteria have been met, the application will be reviewed to determine if the applicant has met the standard set forth in California Penal Code Section 4852.05: "During the period of rehabilitation the person shall live an honest and upright life, shall conduct himself with sobriety and industry, shall exhibit a good moral character, and shall conform to and obey the laws of the land."

Pardons

Any person who has been convicted of an offense in California may apply to the Governor for a pardon. Applications for pardons may be made either by way of an application for a Certificate of Rehabilitation or through a direct traditional pardon application. The procedure utilized will depend on the circumstances of the applicant as explained later.

Once an application for a pardon is filed under either procedure, the Governor reviews the case. The Governor has complete discretion in deciding whether to grant a pardon, and a pardon is not granted to every person who applies. Pardon investigations are conducted for the Governor by the California Board of Prison Terms Investigation Section.

There are no county or state fees for a pardon in California.

Effect of a Pardon

When a Certificate of Rehabilitation or pardon is granted, the California Department of Justice and Federal Bureau of Investigation are notified. These agencies' records are then updated to show that a Certificate of Rehabilitation or a pardon has been granted in regard to the conviction.

A pardon is also filed with the Secretary of State, reported to the Legislature and becomes a matter of public record. Although no effort is made to publicize the pardon application or issuance, there is no guarantee that the issuance of a pardon to a particular person will not become known to the public.

Restoration of Rights

The granting of a pardon entitles the applicant to exercise additional civil and political rights of citizenship. The most frequent reasons people apply for a pardon are for personal satisfaction and for licensing or bonding purposes. Another frequent reason is to enhance employment opportunities, even when no legal disability exists.

A pardon does not seal or expunge the record of the conviction (Section 4852.17 of the California Penal Code). Prior convictions may be considered after the granting of a pardon if the person is subsequently convicted of a new offense.

A person who has been pardoned cannot state that he or she has no record of arrests or convictions. The person can state that he or she has been convicted and has been pardoned.

An ex-felon becomes eligible to vote after being terminated from probation or discharged from parole. (Article II, Section 4 of the California Constitution). A pardon is not necessary to be eligible to vote.

A person who receives a pardon may serve on a trial jury (Section 203(a)(5) of the California Code of Civil Procedure and Section 4852.17 of the California Penal Code).

An ex-felon who receives a full and unconditional pardon can be considered for an appointment to a peace officer position as a county probation officer or state parole agent but cannot hold other peace officer positions (Section 1029 of the California Government Code).

A person convicted of a felony cannot own, possess or have access to any type of firearm including a rifle or shotgun (Section 12021 of the California Penal Code). However, if a full and unconditional pardon is granted by the Governor, the person pardoned may own and possess any type of weapon in California that may lawfully be possessed and owned by other citizens. The Governor cannot restore firearms rights to a person who has been convicted of any offense which involved the use of a dangerous weapon. Pardons for out-of-state residents must specifically state that rights pertaining to firearms are restored. A California pardon does not necessarily permit the possession of weapons under the laws of another state or the federal government. The law pertaining to the restoration of rights to own and possess firearms can be found in Section 4854 of the California Penal Code.

If you do not have a pardon restoring your firearms rights and have access to a firearm of any type, you are in violation of the law. For example, having a firearm registered to a spouse but readily available to you in your place of residence is a violation.

The granting of a pardon does not prevent some licensing agencies from considering the conviction which has been pardoned in its determination of whether a license to practice certain professions should be granted or restored. The law pertaining to the effect of a full pardon on licensing boards can be found in California Penal Code Section 4853.

A California pardon does not pardon convictions suffered in another jurisdiction. A person convicted in another state or in a federal court must apply for a pardon to the other state or the federal government. Federal pardon information can be obtained by writing to the Pardon Attorney, U.S. Department of Justice, Washington, D.C. 20815.

How to Apply for a Pardon

Certificate of Rehabilitation

A Certificate of Rehabilitation is a court order finding that a person who has been convicted of a felony is rehabilitated. If a petition for a Certificate of Rehabilitation is granted, it is forwarded to the Governor by the granting court and constitutes an application for a pardon.

Clear Your Record and Own a Gun

The laws pertaining to the Certificate of Rehabilitation can be found in California Penal Code Sections 4852.01 to 4852.21. Section 4852.2 specifically states that every person other than an individual licensed to practice law in the State of California who solicits or accepts something of value for assisting in the obtaining of a Certificate of Rehabilitation is guilty of a misdemeanor.

Anyone who has been convicted of one or more felonies in California may apply to the superior court in his or her county of residence for a Certificate of Rehabilitation provided a 3-year California residency requirement has been met (Section 4852.06 of the California Penal Code).

The granting of a Certificate of Rehabilitation relieves a person from the sexual offender registration requirement of Penal Code Section 290 (Section 290.5 of the California Penal Code).

Who May Apply

Persons who are eligible to apply for a Certificate of Rehabilitation include those who:

1. Were convicted of a felony and served the sentence in a California state prison; and

   Were discharged on completion of the term or released on parole prior to May 13, 1943; and

   Have not been incarcerated in a state penal institution since release; and

   Present satisfactory evidence of three years residence in California immediately prior to the filing of the petition.

Or

2. Were convicted of a felony, the accusatory pleading of which was dismissed pursuant to Penal Code Section 1203.4; and

   Have not been incarcerated in any penal institution or agency since the dismissal of the accusatory pleading; and

   Are not on probation for the commission of any felony; and

   Present satisfactory evidence of three years residence in California immediately prior to the filing of the petition.

4

Or

3. Were convicted of a felony after May 13, 1943; and

    Were sentenced to state prison; and

    Have completed parole; and

    Present satisfactory evidence of three years residence in California immediately prior to the filing of the petition.

Persons who are ineligible to apply for a Certificate of Rehabilitation include:

1. Those who do not meet the above requirements; or

2. Those who were convicted of misdemeanors only; or

3. Those who are serving a mandatory life parole; or

4. Those committed to prison under a death sentence; or

5. Those persons in the military service.

When to Apply

Persons eligible to petition for a Certificate of Rehabilitation may file the petition once the period of rehabilitation has passed. The period of rehabilitation begins to run upon the discharge of the petitioner from incarceration due to the completion of the term or upon release on probation or parole.

The period of rehabilitation constitutes three years residence in California plus:

1. Four years in the case of a person convicted of violation of California Penal Code Sections 187, 209, 219, 4500, or 12310, or Military and Veterans Code Section 1672(a), or of committing any other offense which carries a life sentence; or

2. Two years in the case of any person convicted of any offense not listed above and which does not carry a life sentence.

Procedure for Applying

The petition must be filed in the superior court of the petitioner's county of residence (Section 4852.06 of the California Penal Code). A Petition for Certificate of Rehabilitation form and a Notice of Filing Petition form can usually be obtained from the county clerk; however, in some counties, the process is handled by the county public defender's office. The petitioner is required to provide notice of the filing to the district attorney of the county of residence and of each county in which the petitioner was convicted of a felony and to the Governor's Office. Felony convictions for which the accusatory pleading was dismissed pursuant to Section 1203.4 of the California Penal Code should be included. This notice must indicate the date and time of the hearing and must be sent at least 30 days before the hearing.

Each person who is eligible to initiate the Certificate of Rehabilitation proceedings is entitled to receive assistance in processing the petition from the county clerk, the county probation officer, the county district attorney, the county public defender or legal aid society, state parole agents, or the Board of Prison Terms. During the court proceedings on the petition, the petitioner may be represented by counsel of his own choosing. If he does not have counsel, he may be represented by the public defender or by the adult probation officer. The court may assign counsel to represent the petitioner if it feels that counsel is needed.

Once a petition is filed, the court will schedule a hearing to consider the petition. Prior to the hearing, the court may require an investigation by the district attorney of the county of residence of any and all matters pertaining to the petitioner. At the hearing, the court may require testimony and the production of records and reports pertaining to the petitioner, the crime of which he was convicted, and his conduct while incarcerated and since release on probation or parole.

If, after the hearing, the court finds that the petitioner has demonstrated rehabilitation and fitness to exercise all political and civil rights, the court will make an order declaring that the petitioner is rehabilitated. A certified copy of the Certificate of Rehabilitation is transmitted to the Governor and becomes an application for a pardon.

Upon receipt of the application, the Governor may request that the Board of Prison Terms conduct a further investigation. Following a review, the Governor may then grant the pardon. If the petitioner has been convicted of more than one felony in separate proceedings, the California Supreme Court must also approve the grant of a pardon.

Traditional Pardon

The traditional pardon procedure is available to those persons who are ineligible to petition for a Certificate of Rehabilitation. This procedure is used primarily, although not exclusively, by California ex-felons who reside out-of-state and are therefore unable to satisfy the residency requirement. The traditional pardon procedure is covered by Sections 4800 to 4813 of the California Penal Code.

Applicants for a traditional pardon must write directly to the Governor's Office at the following address:

>   Governor
>   State Capitol
>   Sacramento, CA 95814
>
>   Attention: Legal Affairs Secretary

The letter should include:

1. Why a pardon is desired or needed;

2. The date and circumstances of all felony offenses of which the applicant was convicted;

3. The dates the applicant was received in prison and released from custody or placed on probation;

4. Name of the applicant, including any aliases, date of conviction, county and case number of conviction if known, prison number, name of parole agent, current address and telephone number; and

5. A brief general statement of employment and activities since conviction or release from custody.

Upon receipt of the letter, the Governor's Legal Affairs staff reviews the information. After the review, the Governor may send the Application for Executive Clemency and Notice of Intention to Apply for Executive Clemency forms to the applicant.

The applicant should complete the Application for Executive Clemency form and have it notarized. In addition, the Notice of Intention to Apply for Executive Clemency should be served on the District Attorney of each county in which the applicant was convicted of a felony. It is suggested that a copy of the application be served on the district attorney along with the notice form.

The acknowledgment of receipt portion of the notice form must be completed and signed by the District Attorney. Both the Application and the completed Notice must then be submitted to the Governor's Office along with a full statement of any compensation paid to any person for assisting in the procurement of a pardon.

Once the formal application is returned, the Governor refers it to the Board of Prison Terms for investigation. After the investigation, the case is presented to the full Board for a decision as to whether to recommend to the Governor that a pardon be granted. The applicant is notified of when the Board will be considering his or her case and he or she is given the opportunity to forward any additional information if desired. Pardon applicants do not attend the pardon consideration meeting. Following the Board meeting, the application, investigation and recommendation are sent to the Governor. Notification of the meeting result is also sent to the applicant.

The Governor reviews all of the information and decides whether to grant a pardon. If the applicant has been convicted of more than one felony in separate proceedings, the California Supreme Court must also approve the grant of a pardon.

There is no requirement that the Governor issue a pardon to an applicant. The length of time needed for the completion of the pardon process cannot be predicted.

California Firearms Rights Recovery

Certificate of Rehabilitation

Computing the Rehabilitation Period

The rehabilitation period begins on the most recent date of release from jail or prison (i.e., release on probation or parole or direct discharge from prison).

There are two categories of rehabilitation periods:

I. If the rehabilitation period began prior to January 1, 1981:

   A. There is a base period of 3 years PLUS,

      1. Thirty days for each year of the current maximum sentence possible under the Determinate Sentence Law (including any enhancements):

         a. For concurrent sentences, the crime with the longest sentence is used.

         b. For consecutive sentences, total the maximum possible number of months for each crime but do not exceed 50 months.

      2. Fifty months for a life sentence.

II. If the rehabilitation period began on or after January 1, 1981:

   A. There is a base period of 3 years PLUS,

      1. Four years if convicted of Penal Code Sections 187, 209, 219, 4500 or 12310, or Military and Veterans Code Section 1672(a), or any other offense which carries a life sentence.

      2. Two years if convicted of any offense not listed in Section 1.

Distributed by: California Board of Prison Terms
Investigation Section
545 Downtown Plaza, Suite 200
Sacramento, California 95814
Telephone: (916) 322-9467

4/91

Clear Your Record and Own a Gun

Chapter 6
Louisiana Firearm Rights Recovery

APPLICATION FOR RIGHT TO BEAR ARMS PERMISSION GIVEN BY PARISH SHERIFF

PUBLIC SAFETY-Louisiana Revised Statute

§14:95.1
 Possession of a firearm or carrying of a concealed weapon by a person convicted of certain felonies.
 A. It is unlawful for any person who has been convicted of first degree murder, manslaughter, aggravated battery, aggravated, forcible, or simple rape, aggravated crime against nature, aggravated kidnapping, aggravated arson, aggravated or simple burglary, armed or simple robbery, burglary of a pharmacy, burglary of an inhabited dwelling, or any violation of the Uniform Controlled Substance Law, [R.S. 40:961, et seq.]to possess a firearm or carry a concealed weapon which is a felony or any crime defined as an attempt of one of the above enumerated offenses under the laws of this state or of the United States, or of any foreign government or country of a crime which, if committed in this state, would be one of the above enumerated crimes, to possess a firearm or carry a concealed weapon. (The word aggravated in most cases means that the use of a weapon was involved in the crime, whether threat or employment).

B. Whoever is found guilty of violating the provisions of this Section (§14:95.1) shall be imprisoned at hard labor for not less than three (3) nor more than ten (10) years without benefit of probation, parole, or suspension of sentence, and be fined not less than one thousand dollars ($1000) nor more than five thousand dollars ($5000).

C. Very important

1. The provision of this section prohibiting the possession of firearms and carrying concealed weapons by persons who have been convicted of certain felonies shall not apply to any person who has not been convicted of any felony for a period of 10 years from the date of completion of sentence, probation, parole, or suspension of sentence.

2. Upon completion of sentence, probation, parole, or suspension of sentence, the convicted felon shall have the right to apply to the sheriff of the parish in which he resides, or in the case of Orleans Parish, the superintendent of police, for a permit to possess firearms. The felon shall be entitled to possess the firearm upon the issuing of the permit.

3. The sheriff or superintendent of police, as the case may be, shall immediately notify the Department of Public Safety in writing of the issuance of each permit granted under this section.

So, after a 10 year period from the date of the completion of sentence, you can ask your local sheriff to allow you to carry a weapon, and he in turn will notify the state.

[Notice: the definition of 'felony' in Louisiana is decidedly different from some other states–in Louisiana, it's described as, "any crime for which an offender may be sentenced to death or hard labor." In most states it is any crime for which the sentence can be incarceration for a year or more.

LOUISIANA PARDON(S)

Definition of Pardon:

" The remission by the chief executive (Governor) of a state or nation (president) of a punishment which a person convicted of a crime has been sentenced to undergo."

Basically, it's asking the governor of your state or the president of the United States to forgive your crime, and restore all of your citizenship rights, including the right to bear arms. Either of those entities have the authoritative power to grant civil rights, depending on the type of crime committed, federal or state.

LOUISIANA CODE OF CRIMINAL PROCEDURE
PARDON AND REPRIEVE

R.S.§15:572

Powers of the governor to grant reprieves and pardons-automatic pardon for first offender.

    A. The governor may grant reprieves to persons convicted of offenses against the state and, upon recommendation of the Board of Pardons, as hereinafter provided for by this part, may commute sentences, pardon those convicted of an offense against the state, and remit fines and forfeitures imposed for such offense.

    B. First offender (never before having a felony record) never previously convicted of a felony shall be pardoned automatically upon completion of his sentence without recommendation of the board of pardons and without any action by the governor.

    C. For the purpose of this Section, "First Offender" means a person convicted within this state of a felony but never previously convicted of a felony within this state or convicted under the laws of any other state or of the United States or of any foreign government or country of a crime which, if committed in this state, would have been a felony, regardless of any previous convictions for any misdemeanors. Convictions in other jurisdictions which do not have counterparts, (are not like anything Louisiana has in its Code of Criminal Procedure) in this state will be classified according to the laws of the jurisdiction of the conviction.

    D. On the day that an individual completes his sentence, the Division of Probation and Parole of the Department of Corrections, after satisfying itself that:

1. The individual is a first offender as described herein
2. The individual has completed his sentence

The Department of Corrections shall issue a certificate recognizing and proclaiming that the petitioner (you) is fully pardoned of the offense, and that he has all rights of citizenship and franchise, (including the right to bear arms) and the division of probation/parole) shall transmit a copy of the certificate to the individual and to the Clerk of Court in and for the parish where the conviction occurred. This copy shall be filed in the record of the proceedings in which the conviction was obtained. However, once an automatic pardon is granted under this section, the individual who received such pardon shall not be entitled to receive another automatic pardon.

(Note: Because the word petitioner is used in this statute, it would be very important that you check your records with the Clerk of Court to see if your automatic pardon was indeed filed. If you don't see it, ask the Clerk of Court to find out why it's not there.

PARDON BY GOVERNOR
STATE OF LOUISIANA

Beyond the 10 year waiting limit for the restoring of the right to bear arms, are several other methods. One of them is the full pardon method, by applying to the state governor. This can not only restore your weapons rights, but all other citizenship rights as well. It can be a lengthy and time consuming process, especially if you have to do it more than once, as I did.

In Louisiana, to begin the process of obtaining a pardon from the governor, it is critical that you start immediately. As stated, it can take time. To get an application for pardon, write to:

State of Louisiana
Department of Public Safety & Corrections
Board of Pardons
504 Mayflower Street
Baton Rouge, Louisiana
70802

Or, you can call them and request an application for pardon, and they will mail you one. Telephone number: (504) 342-5421.

A set of the pardon board rules for the application is in this book. Please, follow them closely. After your application is received, a hearing will be set for a specific date. The results of that hearing will go directly to the governor. Before you do anything else, be advised that it is important that you get as much support as you can muster from family, employers, friends, politicians, educators, etc.

Notice that the rules require that you run a three (3) day ad in your local newspaper. Keep your receipt when you run the ad, you will need to prove that it was done. The purpose of the ad is to let victims or the victim's family know that you're applying for pardon. They have the right to be at your hearing, too. By the way, you can apply for a partial pardon in which you can get all of your rights restored except the right to bear arms. That is not what you want.

When you're requesting the application for pardon, refer to the Louisiana Revised Statute 15:572.4, under Louisiana Statutory Criminal Law and Procedure. For your convenience, there are two of my own pardons in this book. The first one does not have the right to bear arms. (Dated November 18, 1991.) The second one, dated April 14, 1992, does have the right to bear arms included. Ordinarily, it would have been required that I wait a year until I could have reapplied for pardon, but given that the pardon board had voted unanimously to restore all of my rights, and specifically the right to bear arms, I sent the board recommendation to the new governor, just elected. In turn, I was granted the weapons right. Added to the Ohio relief from disability, that makes me legal to carry weapons anywhere in the United States–(misdemeanors, as on my record, do not block the right to bear arms). Copies of pardons from Governor Roemer and Governor Edwards are enclosed). Persistence is the name of the game in any post conviction relief. During my third pardon board hearing, I was asked by a board member what I would do if I wasn't granted a full pardon. I looked at him and the rest of the board members and said that they would see me again, in a year, then again the next year. I meant it.

EXPUNGEMENT
Erasure of Criminal Record In Louisiana

Another method of restoring the right to bear arms is expungement-which in effect erases your criminal record as if nothing ever happened. Many states have this law, usually for first offenders or juveniles. I am told by some legal eagles that an expungement does not return your right to bear arms-but I question the validity of that statement, if you don't have an existing record for the law enforcement officials to find, how can you not have the right to bear arms?

LOUISIANA REVISED STATUTE

Note: Only pertinent sections of the statutes are used in this book. For complete statute contact your local law library.

§44:9

Records of violations of municipal ordinances and state statutes classified as a felony:

Part B:

Any criminal court of record in which there was a nolle prosequi, (no prosecution) an acquittal, (found not guilty), or dismissal (charges dropped by court) of any offense, whether misdemeanor or felony, shall at the time of discharge of a person from its control, enter an order annulling, cancelling, or rescinding the record of arrest and disposition, and further ordering the destruction of the arrest record, and order of disposition. Upon entry of such an order the person against whom the arrest, unless otherwise provided for in this section, shall be treated in all respects as not having been arrested.

Part C.

(1.) Any person who has been arrested for the violation of a state statute which is classified as a felony may make a written (sample and actual motion enclosed) to the district court for the parish in which he was arrested for expungement of the arrest record if the time limit (prescription) of the institution (starting the prosecution) has expired, and no prosecution has been instituted.

If you were charged and arrested, or just charged, and the time limit for the D.A.'s office has run out for bringing you to court, (usually six months-misdemeanors- and a year for felonies) you can motion the court to expunge your record.

(2.) If, after a contradictory hearing with the arresting agency, (those who filed the charges against you have the chance in court to explain and argue why you should not get an expungement) the court finds that the mover (you who filed the motion for expungement) is entitled to the relief sought for any of the above reasons, it shall order all law enforcement agencies to expunge (erase) same (the arrest record and disposition) in accordance herewith. However, the arresting agency may preserve the name and address of the person and the facts of the case for investigative purposes only.

For the purpose of investigation means that if another crime is committed that was similar to yours, the police can go back and look at it. Basically, the record is "sealed" without public access. However, the statute itself states that the record must be destroyed. The arresting agency can keep it under lock and key, but it remains that the case must be considered as if it never happened.

Please, take special notice that this is the first time that misdemeanor and felony records are mentioned together, under Statute 44.9 (copy of 44.9 enclosed)

What if there was a way, if your case didn't fall under any of the criteria listed as necessary to file for an expungement–the nolle pros, the acquittal, or the dismissal– to get it into court and still get the record erased? In Louisiana, (and other states) you can. First, you get your case dismissed:

Code of Criminal Procedure (Louisiana) Articles 893 & 894:

Art. 893 Suspension of sentence & probation in felony cases.

A. When it appears that the best interest of the public and of the defendant (you) will be served, the court, after issuance of a felony conviction, shall, for the first conviction only, place the defendant on probation, and suspend the sentence.

C. If the sentence consists of both a fine and imprisonment, the court may impose the fine and suspend the sentence, and place the defendant on probation.

E. When the imposition of sentence has been suspended by the court, as authorized by this article, and that court finds at the conclusion of the probationary period (that it was satisfactory), the court may set aside the conviction and dismiss the prosecution, and the dismissal shall have the same effect as acquittal, except that said conviction may be considered a first offense (that's a hint) and provide the basis for—. (This article does indeed dismiss the charges, allowing you to go back to court for expungement.)

MISDEMEANORS UNDER Article 894

(4.) The Court may suspend– sentence.
    (B.) Follow guidelines under 893), and the "dismissal shall have the same effect as acquittal—".

The following pages consist of copies of samples and actual expungements.

Louisiana Firearms Rights Recovery

STATE OF LOUISIANA
or
CITY OF LAFAYETTE)   I   CITY COURT OF LAFAYETTE

VERSUS   I   STATE OF LOUISIANA

(Name of Defendant)   I   DOCKET NUMBER _____

* *

MOTION TO SET ASIDE AND DISMISS PROSECUTION

ON motion of (Name of Defendant), through his undersigned counsel and on a showing that defendant, (Name of Defendant), was convicted after entering a plea of no contest on _____ (Date) _____ to a violation of, (Put name of charge and statute number or city ordinance number, example OWI, L. R. S. 14:98 or Simple Battery, Code of Ordinances, Section 10-67), and on the further showing that the defendant was ordered on __(Date)__ to pay a fine of $____ plus costs, and serve a period of ____ days in the parish jail, said days suspended upon good behavior, and complaince with conditions of unsupervised probation for ____ months and that the defendant has not been convicted of any other offense during the period of the suspended sentence and probation and that, pursuant to Article 894 of the Louisiana Code of Criminal Procedure, the Court may therefore set the said conviction aside and dismiss the prosecution and that the Assistant District Attorney (or City Prosecutor) and the Chief of Police have no opposition to this motion as evidenced by their signatures below:

IT IS HEREBY ORDERED AND DECREED that the conviction against the defendant, _(Name of Defendant)_ , DOB: (Date of Birth), of (Name of Charge and Statute number or Ordinance number) under the above referenced docket number is hereby set aside, except the fine and court costs previously paid, which shall be considered forfeited, and the prosecution is hereby dismissed.

ORDERED this ____ day of _____, 19___, at Lafayette, Louisiana.

                                                    _____
                                                    JUDGE, DIVISION " "
                                                    CITY COURT OF LAFAYETTE, LOUISIANA

_____
MOVER'S SIGNATURE

_____
ASSISTANT DISTRICT ATTORNEY
(OR CITY PROSECUTOR)

_____
CHIEF OF POLICE

Clear Your Record and Own a Gun

STATE OF LOUISIANA | I | CITY COURT OF LAFAYETTE, LOUISIANA
(OR CITY OF LAFAYETTE)

VERSUS | I | STATE OF LOUISIANA

(Name of Defendant) | I | DOCKET NUMBER _____

* * * * * * * * * * * * * * * SAMPLE * * * * * * * * * * * * * * * * * *

ORDER OF EXPUNGEMENT

  On motion of __(Name of Defendant)__ , appearing through his undersigned counsel, upon considering the foregoing petition, and the law and evidence being in favor of Defendant, pursuant to L.R.S. 44:9;

  IT IS ORDERED, ADJUSGED AND DECREED that all agencies and law enforcement officers having any record of the arrest, whether on microfilm, computer card or tape, and on any other photographic, electronic or mechanical method of storing data, destroy any record of arrest, photograph, fingerprint or any information of any and all kinds or descriptions relating to this charge;

  IT IS FURTHER ORDERED, ADJUDGED AND DECREED that the Custodian of such records file a sworn addidavit in the City Court of Lafayette, Louisiana, that all records have been destroyed and that no notations or references have been retained in the agency's central repository which will or might lead to the showing that any record was on file with any agency or law enforcement office.

  IT IS FURTHER ORDERED, ADJUDGED AND DECREED that the issuing agency be entitled to keep a copy of their affidavit to this Court but said affidavit shall not be a public record or open for public inspection, but rather kept under lock and key and maintained only for internal record keeping purposes to preserve the integrity of said agency's files and shall not be used for any investigatory purposes.

  ORDERED this _____ day of _____, 19___ at Lafayette, Louisiana.

_____
JUDGE, DIVISION " "
CITY COURT OF LAFAYETTE, LOUISIANA

_____
MOVER'S SIGNATURE

Louisiana Firearms Rights Recovery

CITY OF LAFAYETTE   : CITY COURT OF LAFAYETTE
VERSUS   : PARISH OF LAFAYETTE
                           : STATE OF LOUISIANA

ORDER REQUIRING EXPUNGEMENT OF ARREST RECORD

Considering the foregoing motion filed in accordance with LSA-R.S. 44:9, the Court finding that the mover is entitled to the relief sought, for the reasons contained in the foregoing motion:

IT IS ORDERED that all agencies and law enforcement offices, including the City of Lafayette Police Department, the Lafayette Parish Sheriff's Department, the Louisiana Department of Public Safety and Corrections, the Office of State Police, and the Louisiana Bureau of Criminal Identification and Information having any record of the arrest of the defendant,

whether on microfilm, computer card or tape, or on any other photographic, electronic, or mechanical method of storing data, to destroy any record of arrest, photograph, fingerprint, or any other information of any and all kinds or descriptions;

IT IS FURTHER ORDERED that the custodians of records of each of the agencies or law enforcement offices referred to above and any other such agencies and law enforcement offices shall file a sworn affidavit to the effect that the records of arrest of the defendant,   have been destroyed and that no notations or references have been retained in the agency's central repository which will or might lead to the inference that any record ever was on file with any agency or law enforcement office; and

IT IS FURTHER ORDERED that the original of the affidavit referred to above shall be kept by this Court and a copy shall be retained by the affiant agency, which said copy shall

Clear Your Record and Own a Gun

not be a public record and shall not be open for public inspection, but rather shall be kept under lock and key and maintained only for internal record keeping purposes to preserve the integrity of said agency's files and shall not be used for any investigative purpose.

THIS ORDER SIGNED in Lafayette, Louisiana, on this _____ day of _____, 198___.

_____
JUDGE

PLEASE SERVE:

Lafayette City Police Department, Records Custodian
Lafayette Parish Sheriff's Department, Records Custodian
Louisiana Department of Public Safety and Corrections,
    Records Custodian
Louisiana Office of State Police, Records Custodian
Louisiana Bureau of Criminal Identification and
    Information, Records Custodian

SAMPLE

STATE OF LOUISIANA	*	(your) JUDICIAL DISTRICT
VERSUS	*	DOCKET NO. (YOURS)
(YOUR NAME)	*	PARISH OF (YOURS)

****

MOTION TO EXPUNGE

The verified petition of (your name) (complete address), respectfully avers that the following allegations, together with the attached concurrence of the Office of the District Attorney of (your parish) support the prayer of or relief requested in this Motion To Expunge the entirety of the criminal proceedings in the above captioned and numbered cause.

1.

On (date of charge) the defendant was charged with a violation of (state charge and statute from your record).

2.

That the said (your name) pursuant to LSA-R.S.44.9, is entitled to expungment of the arrest record and criminal proceedings on file with the (name of parish sheriff's department) and accordingly,

IT IS ORDERED, ADJUDGED AND DECREED that all Agencies and Law Enforcement Offices having any record of the arrest of (your name) for (your charge) destroy any and all records of arrest, photograph, fingerprint, or any other information of any and all kinds of descriptions relating to the arrest of the said (your name) and shall file an affidavit to the effect that the records have been destroyed and that no notations or references have been retained in the Agencies' Central Repository which will lead or might lead to inference that any record ever was on file with any agency or law enforcement office.

(Name of city or town of court,) Louisiana, this ____ day of _____, 199-.

_____
DISTRICT JUDGE

Louisiana Firearms Rights Recovery

STATE OF LOUISIANA　　　　　　　15TH JUDICIAL DISTRICT COURT
VERSUS　　　　　　　　　　　　　DOCKET NO.: 49155 & 48797
WILLIAM A. RINEHART　　　　　　PARISH OF LAFAYETTE, LOUISIANA

* *

MOTION TO EXPUNGE

The verified petition of **WILLIAM A. RINEHART**, 930 Guilbeau Road #39, Lafayette, Louisiana, respectfully avers that the following allegations, together with the attached concurrence of the Office of the District Attorney of Lafayette Parish, Louisiana, support the prayer of or relief requested and contained in this Motion to Expunge the entirety of the criminal proceedings in the above captioned and numbered cause.

1.

On May 29, 1983, the defendant was charged with a violation of R.S. 14:62, Simple Burglary, and on August 29, 1983, was charged with R.S. 14:125, False Swearing.

2.

That the said **WILLIAM A. RINEHART** pursuant to LSA-R.S. 44:9, is entitled to expungement of the arrest record and criminal proceedings on file with the Lafayette Parish Sheriff's Department, and accordingly,

IT IS ORDERED, ADJUDGED AND DECREED that all Agencies and Law Enforcement Offices having any record of the arrest of **WILLIAM A. RINEHART** for R.S. 14:62 Simple Burglary and R.S. 14:125 destroy any and all records of arrest, photograph, fingerprint, or any other information of any and all kinds of descriptions relating to the arrest of the said **WILLIAM A. RINEHART** and shall file an affidavit to the effect that the records have been destroyed and that no notations or references have been retained in the Agencies' central repository which will lead or might lead inference that any record ever was on file with any agency or law enforcement office.

Lafayette, Louisiana this _14_ day of _December_, 1988.

DISTRICT JUDGE

FILED this _14th_ day of _Dec_, 19 _88_
TRUE COPY ATTEST, Lafayette, La.

BY, Clerk of Court

Original sent to Judge Gautreaux 12-9-88

CLEAR YOUR RECORD AND OWN A GUN

MARCH 10, 1992   JUDGE MICHOT

Court met this date pursuant to adjournment with the Honorable Patrick L. Michot, Judge presiding; Jackie LeBeouf, Court Reporter; Robin Rhodes, Janet Perrodin, Michael Harson, Assistant District Attorneys; Patricia Guilbeau, Deputy Clerk of Court; Harris LeBlanc, Harvey Mouton, Deputy Sheriffs; all being in attendance.

STATE OF LOUISIANA   )   **MOTION TO EXPUNGE**
VS   )   The accused was present in open Court,
WILLIAM ARTHUR RINEHART)   but was not represented by counsel. A
Motion to Expunge was previously granted and a partial return was filed from 3rd Circuit as 48797 and 49155, which the Court stated State Police and FBI records were not expunged.

The State objected to the Expungement.

The Court ordered State Police and FBI to expunge records in 49155 and 48797.

WHEREUPON COURT THEN ADJOURNED

3/20/92

HONORABLE PATRICK L. MICHOT, JUDGE

Louisiana Firearms Rights Recovery

STATE OF LOUISIANA   15TH JUDICIAL DISTRICT COURT

VS   PARISH OF LAFAYETTE, LOUISIANA

WILLIAM ARTHUR RINEHART   DOCKET NO. 49155, 48797

* *

TO: Lafayette City Police Dept, Records Custodian, 107 East Convent
Lafayette, Lousiiana

Lafayette Parish Sheriff, Records Custodian, Lafayette, La.

Louisiana Department of Public Safety and Corrections, Records Custodian, 209 S. Foster Drive, Baton Rouge, La.

Louisiana State Police, Records Custodian, 265 S Foster Drive Baton Rouge, La.

Louisiana Office of State Police, Lafayette, Lousiiana

Louisiana Bureau of Criminal Identification and Inform., Records Custodian, 1885 Wooddale Blvd, Baton Rouge, La.

Federal Bureau of Investigation, Office of Criminal Indentification and Information, Records Custodian, FBI Headquarters, Washington, D. C. 20535

District Attorney, Lafayette, Louisiana

Attorney of Record:_____

_____

YOU ARE HEREBY SERVED WITH A CERTIFIED COPY OF   MINUTE ENTRY
_____.

WITNESS THE HONORABLE JUDGES OF THE 15TH JUDICIAL DISTRICT COURT,

THIS   23rd   day of   March   , 19 92

                                             [signature]
                                         DEPUTY CLERK OF COURT

Clear Your Record and Own a Gun

4-1992 15:41   3184432625   GRAVEL BRADY LAW FIRM   P.2

"Exhibit A"

STATE OF LOUISIANA
DEPARTMENT OF PUBLIC SAFETY AND CORRECTIONS
BOARD OF PARDONS
504 Mayflower Street
Baton Rouge, La. 70802
Phone (504) 342-5421

BUDDY ROEMER, GOVERNOR   BRUCE LYNN, SECRETARY

June 26, 1990

TO THE HONORABLE BUDDY ROEMER, GOVERNOR, STATE OF LOUISIANA:

On application of: RINEHART, WILLIAM   W/M DOB 7/20/45
                    OUT   FBI # 767115F
                    File # 16797   SID # 935740

Offender Class: Second
Offense: S/Burglary and False Swearing
Sentenced: December 8, 1983 - 3 yrs. P.J. & 3 Mo. P.J.
Judicial District: Fifteenth - Lafayette Parish

Applicant was sentenced as the result of pleading guilty of the offenses listed above. His case was heard before the Board of Pardons on June 19, 1990. He has satisfied his sentences and presently resides in Lafayette, Louisiana.

The Lafayette City Police Department opposes restoration of firearms privileges and a pardon. The District Attorney only opposes restoration of firearms privileges. The Sheriff has no objection to a pardon or restoration of firearms privileges.

Mr. Rinehart has made strong efforts toward rehabilitation and all indications point to success. He expects to graduate from college soon and having a pardon would enhance his chances of obtaining a suitable position. He has strong family and community support.

The Board recommends that applicant be granted a PARDON AND RESTORATION OF ALL CIVIL AND CITIZENSHIP RIGHTS, INCLUDING THE RIGHT TO OWN, POSSESS, RECEIVE, SHIP OR TRANSPORT FIREARMS.

Respectfully submitted,

YVONNE G. CAMPBELL, CHAIRMAN

Louisiana Firearms Rights Recovery

UDDY ROEMER
GOVERNOR

State of Louisiana
OFFICE OF THE GOVERNOR
Baton Rouge
70804-9004

POST OFFICE BOX 94004
(504) 342-7015
FAX NO. (504) 342-0909

April 18, 1991

Mr. William Rinehart
300 Spruce Street
Lafayette, Louisiana 70506

Dear Mr. Rinehart:

After carefully reviewing and considering the recommendation of the Pardon Board and all matters presented in your case, I have decided to grant you a pardon.

Enclosed please find the official copy of your pardon signed on November 18, 1991.

Sincerely,

Buddy Roemer
Governor

BR:by

Enclosure

Clear Your Record and Own a Gun

Executive Department

To Whom It May Concern:

Whereas, At a session of the Honorable the Fifteenth Judicial District Court in and for the Parish of Lafayette, held on the 18th day of December, 1983 WILLIAM RINEHART was tried and convicted of the crime of simple burglary and false swearing and for said offense was sentenced by His Honor, the Judge of said court, to three (3) years in the Parish Jail and six months in the Parish Jail.

And, Whereas, upon the recommendation of the Honorable Board of Pardons, I have thought proper to grant a pardon and restoration of all civil and citizenship rights to William Rinehart, excluding the right to own, possess, receive, ship and transport firearms.

Now, Therefore, I, BUDDY ROEMER , Governor of the State of Louisiana, by virtue of the powers vested in me by the Constitution, do hereby grant a pardon and restoration of all civil and citizenship rights to William Rinehart, excluding the right to own, possess, receive, ship and transport firearms.

and do hereby direct you to act accordingly, and for so doing this shall be your sufficient warrant and authority.

Given under my signature and the Great Seal of the State of Louisiana, at the City of Baton Rouge, this 18th day of November , A.D., 19 91

Governor

By The Governor:

Secretary of State

LOUISIANA FIREARMS RIGHTS RECOVERY

EDWIN W. EDWARDS
GOVERNOR

State of Louisiana
OFFICE OF THE GOVERNOR
Baton Rouge
70804-9004

POST OFFICE BOX 94004
(504) 342-7015

April 14, 1992

Mr. William Arthur Rinehart
300 Spruce Drive, #204
Lafayette, LA   70506

Dear Mr. Rinehart:

    After carefully reviewing and considering the recommendation of the Pardon Board and all matters presented in your case, I have decided to grant a pardon to you and restoration of all civil and citizenship rights, including the right to own, possess, receive, ship and transport firearms.

    Enclosed please find the official copy of your parole eligibility signed on April 14, 1992.

Sincerely,

Edwin W. Edwards
Governor

EWE:kjp
Enclosure

Clear Your Record and Own a Gun

Executive Department

TO WHOM IT MAY CONCERN:

Whereas, At a session of the Honorable the Fifteenth Judicial District Court in and for the Parish of Lafayette

held on the 18th *day of* December, 1983   WILLIAM RINEHART *was tried and convicted of the crime of* Simple Burglary and False Swearing *and for said offense was sentenced by His Honor, the Judge of said court, to* three (3) years in the Parish Jail and six (6) months in the Parish Jail.

And, Whereas, upon the recommendation of the Honorable Board of Pardons, I have thought proper to grant a pardon and restoration of all civil and citizenship rights to William Rinehart, including the right to own, possess, receive, ship and transport firearms.

Now, Therefore, I, EDWIN EDWARDS *, Governor of the State of Louisiana, by virtue of the powers vested in me by the Constitution, do hereby grant a* pardon and restoration of all civil and citizenship rights to William Rinehart, including the right to own, possess, receive, ship and transport firearms,

and I hereby direct you to act accordingly, and for so doing this shall be your sufficient warrant and authority.

Given under my signature and the Great Seal of the State of Louisiana, at the City of Baton Rouge, this 14th *day of* April *, A.D. 19* 92.

Governor

By The Governor:

Secretary of State

FORM 509 (R 10/72)

Chapter 7
Ohio Firearm Rights Recovery

Ohio has a criminal law statute, Title 29, the Ohio Criminal Code, that allows for the application of the right to bear arms, without applying for a pardon. It is called a relief from disability (of not being legally able to have firearms). A copy of my own relief from disability is enclosed. The statute:

§2923.14

(A) Any person who, solely by reason of his disability under division (a)(2) or (3) of section 2923.13 of the revised code (fugitive from justice, under indictment for a felony of violence, juvenile delinquent, drug trafficking, drug dependent, chronic alcoholic, or mentally incompetent) may apply to the Court of Common Pleas in the county where he resides for relief from such prohibition. (Anyone can apply).

(B) The application shall recite the following:

(1) All indictments, convictions, or adjudications upon which the applicant's disability is based, the sentence imposed and served, and probation, parole, or partial or conditional pardon granted, or other disposition of each case;

(2) Facts showing the applicant to be a fit subject for relief under this section.

(C) A copy of the application shall be served on the county prosecutor, who shall cause the matter to be investigated, and shall raise before the court such objections to granting relief as the investigation reveals.

(D) Upon hearing, the court may grant the applicant relief (return the right to bear arms), if all of the following apply:

(1) The applicant has been fully discharged from imprisonment, probation, and parole, or, if he is under indictment, has been released on bail or recognizance;

(2) The applicant has led a law-abiding life since his discharge or release, and appears likely to continue to do so;

(3) The applicant is not otherwise prohibited by law from acquiring, having, or using firearms.

(E) Costs (court costs paid by applicant-this is a civil proceeding)

(F) (2) Applies only with respect to firearms lawfully acquired, possessed, carried, or used by the applicant."

The difference between this restoration of the right to bear arms and a pardon–this lets you buy, sell, or carry or use weapons–but restores only that right, and this motion is done in the County Common Pleas Court, not by the governor. It is limited to that entity. (See author's granted relief from disability, and the comments of the prosecutor.)

(A note on relief from disability-the Ohio felony was committed in 1973, but I didn't apply for my relief from disability until 1992, some nineteen years later. Living in Louisiana, I made the motion for relief by mail. However, prior to the motion, I had applied for full pardon in Ohio, and was denied, unanimously. Then, after being granted the relief, I applied again for full pardon, questioning the common sense of giving me the right to bear arms, but not giving me a full pardon. I could carry a gun, but I didn't have all of my civil rights. This time I received the full pardon, by unanimous vote).

The following pages contain documentation of the author's relief from disability grant.

Ohio Firearm Rights Recovery

LEE C. FALKE
PROSECUTING ATTORNEY OF
MONTGOMERY COUNTY
5th Floor
Dayton-Montgomery County Courts Building
301 West Third Street
Dayton, Ohio 45402
(513) 225-5757

CRIMINAL DIVISION
James M. Connell
Angela Frydman
Helen O. Evans
Linda L. Howland
James D. Cole
George B. Patricoff
David M. Franceschelli
William F. Randolph
Sandra K. Hobson
Gregory J. Corbin
Richard W. Divine
Steven J. Ring
Richard D. Hanes
William O. Cass
James L. Morford
William E. Fischer
Greg R. Noble
Paul A. Folfas
Thomas R. Schiff
R. Casey Daganhardt
Arvin S. Miller III
Raymond Dundes

CAREER CRIMINAL UNIT
Leon J. Daidone

GRAND JURY/INTAKE DIVISION
George A. Katchmer
Ellen C. Weprin

JUVENILE COURT
225-4253
Debra Bonifas Armanini
J. David Turner
Josie Olsvig Harr
Carol S. Kidwell
Janet Sorrell
Thaddeus Armstead
Pamela Drucker
Jenifer Wilhelm

APPELLATE DIVISION
225-4117
Ted E. Millspaugh
Carley-Jean Ingram
Walter F. Ruf
Lorine M. Reid
Rebecca Cochran

VICTIM/WITNESS DIVISION
225-5623
Mary Hurt
Rhonda Barner
Lisa C. Edwards
Ada I. Scruggs
Sue Rytel
Sandra Hunt
Beverly Harris

CONSUMER FRAUD DIVISION
225-4747
Robert A. Skinner
Richard A. F. Lipowicz

INVESTIGATORS
Donald R. Otto
Steven W. Longo
Susan Finch

OFFICE MANAGER
Gregg G. Findlay

CASE MANAGEMENT DIVISION
Sandy Dodge

ADMINISTRATIVE ASSISTANTS
Sherri Richardson
Tim Adams

May 15, 1992

DENNIS J. LANGER
First Assistant
MATHIAS H. HECK, JR.
Chief Trial Counsel
TRIAL COUNSEL
John M. Slavens
James R. Levinson

William A. Rinehart
300 Spruce Drive, #204
Lafayette, Louisiana 70506

Re: Case Number: 73-CR-1052
    Motion for Relief of Disability

Dear Mr. Rinehart:

Enclosed please find a certified copy of the ENTRY GRANTING RELIEF FROM DISABILITY filed in the Montgomery County Court of Common Pleas on May 14, 1992.

Very truly yours,

LEE C. FALKE,
Prosecuting Attorney

By _____
STEVEN J. RING
Assistant Prosecuting Attorney

Enclosure

CLEAR YOUR RECORD AND OWN A GUN

IN THE COMMON PLEAS COURT OF MONTGOMERY COUNTY, OHIO

CRIMINAL DIVISION

STATE OF OHIO : CASE NO. 73-CR-1052

      Plaintiff : (Judge Dodge)

  - vs - :

WILLIAM ARTHUR RINEHART : **ENTRY GRANTING RELIEF FROM DISABILITY**

      Defendant :

****

    Upon the written Motion of the Defendant herein, the Court having reviewed the Prosecutor's Response to Defendant's Motion for Relief from Disability pursuant to Ohio Revised Code Section 2923.14, the Court hereby finds that the Defendant herein has been fully discharged from imprisonment, probation, and parole; the Defendant herein has led a law abiding life since his discharge or release, and appears likely to continue to do so; the Defendant herein is not otherwise prohibited by law from acquiring, having or using firearms.

    WHEREFORE, it is the ORDER of the Court that the Defendant herein with respect solely to the indictments, convictions, or adjudications recited in the Defendant's application is hereby relieved of disability. It is the further order of the Court that this relief from disability applies only with respect to firearms lawfully acquired, possessed, carried, or used by the Defendant herein, and said relief from disability does not apply with respect to dangerous ordnance. Further, the Court orders that the costs of this proceeding shall be charged as in other civil case, and taxed to the Defendant/Applicant herein.

    This relief from disability may be revoked by the Court at any time for good cause shown and upon notice to the Defendant.

    This relief from disability is automatically void upon the commission, by the Defendant/Applicant, of any offense embraced by Division (A)(2) or (3) of Section 2923.13 of the Ohio Revised Code, or upon the applicant's becoming one of the class of persons named in Division (A)(1), (4) or (5) of such section.

Ohio Firearm Rights Recovery

SO ORDERED.

/s/ Richard Dodge
HON. RICHARD S. DODGE

LEE C. FALKE,
Prosecuting Attorney

By /s/ Steven J. Ring
STEVEN J. RING
Assistant Prosecuting Attorney
Supreme Court No. 0015129

copies to: Steven J. Ring, Assistant Prosecuting Attorney
William A. Rinehart, 300 Spruce Drive, No. 204,
Lafayette, Louisiana 70506

I hereby certify this to be a true and correct copy.
Witness my hand and seal this 14 day of May 1992.

_____, CLERK
Clerk of Common Pleas
Court of Montgomery County, Ohio
By Sharon Papp
Deputy

OHIO PARDONS

Unlike the presidential pardons which don't use a pardon board, and the California pardons, which use the courts, the state of Ohio does have and uses the Adult Parole Authority as an intermediary between the courts and the governor. The adult parole board serves as a board to hear applications for pardons & paroles.

APPLICATION FOR EXECUTIVE PARDON
Ohio Criminal

Code §2967.07,
All applications for pardon— shall be made in writing to the Adult Parole Authority. Upon the filing of such application, or when directed by the governor in any case, a thorough investigation into the propriety of granting a pardon— shall be made by (that) authority, which shall report in writing to the governor a brief statement of the facts in the case, together with the recommendation of the authority for or against the granting of a pardon, —and the records or minutes relating to the case." (Contact Ohio Adult Parole Authority for application for pardon).

EFFECTS OF UNCONDITIONAL PARDON

§2967.04
(B) An unconditional pardon relieves the person to whom it is granted of all disabilities (including the right to bear arms) arising out of the conviction or convictions from which it is granted. For purposes of this section, unconditional pardon includes a conditional pardon with respect to which all conditions have been performed or have transpired.

RIGHTS OF CITIZENSHIP RESTORED AFTER TERMINATION OF PROBATION

§2951.09

When a defendant on probation is brought before a judge, such judge shall immediately inquire into the conduct of the defendant and may terminate the probation. When the ends of Justice will be served and the good conduct of the person so held warrants it, the judge terminates the person's probation, and the defendant thereupon shall be discharged. If the defendant has been convicted of or has pleaded guilty to a felony, the judge of the court of common pleas may restore to the defendant his rights of citizenship (which also restores the right to arms), of which such convict may or shall have been deprived by reason of his conviction—and if the court makes such order of restoration to citizenship, an entry shall be made.

(An example of this is enclosed–the author had left the state of Ohio, and had not been rearrested, but his probation had remained in effect until the probation department decided to close his case-and withdraw his capias-for which he could have been arrested for leaving the state.) But, when they did close the case, rights of citizenship were automatically restored, the warrant for his arrest ceased to exist, and right to bear arms has been in possession of the author ever since. The sad part of it is, the court never notified the author that his rights had been restored until years later, and only when he had taken it to court.

The following pages contain the author's restoration of rights, withdrawal of capias, and warrant of pardon.

Clear Your Record and Own a Gun

COURT OF COMMON PLEAS
GENERAL DIVISION
MONTGOMERY COUNTY COURTS BUILDING
41 NORTH PERRY STREET
DAYTON, OHIO 45422-2150

RICHARD S. DODGE
JUDGE

AREA CODE 513
225-4376

April 21, 1993

William Arthur Rinehart
300 Spruce Drive, #204
Lafayette, Louisianna 70506

RE: Motion for Restoration of Rights of
    Citizenship - Ohio Revised Code
    Section 2951.09

Dear Mr. Rinehart:

On April 14, 1993, the Court received your Motion for Restoration of Rights of Citizenship, Ohio Revised Code, Section 2951.09.

Upon review of your record, the Court granted an Administrative Termination on August 16, 1983, which closed interest in this case and restored your rights of citizenship. I have enclosed a copy of this entry for your records.

I wish you much success in your pursuit of rehabilitation.

Sincerely,

Richard S. Dodge
Judge

Enclosure

cc: Grafton S. Payne, II, Director
    James E. Dare, Division Manager

The Adult Probation Department
IN THE COURT OF COMMON PLEAS, MONTGOMERY COUNTY, OHIO

The State of Ohio
    Plaintiff

Case No.: 73-CR-1052

Charge: Attempted Breaking and Entering N/S

-vs-

WILLIAM A. RINEHART
    Defendant

WITHDRAWAL OF CAPIAS
ADMINISTRATIVE TERMINATION
NUNC PRO TUNC 12/31/78

It is the Order of the Court in the interest of the public and the Defendant that the probationary status of the Defendant be terminated, and the above case closed.

All outstanding monies on the above case are waived for good cause shown.

APPROVED:

JUDGE
Carl D. Kessler

DIRECTOR OF PROBATION
James F. Wichtman

DIVISION MANAGER
Elizabeth Baxter

7/27/83

CLEAR YOUR RECORD AND OWN A GUN

GEORGE V. VOINOVICH
Governor of said State

To all to whom these Presents shall come, Greeting:

Whereas, at the ___October___ term of the Court of Common Pleas held in and for the County of ___Montgomery___, in the year of our Lord One Thousand Nine Hundred and ___Seventy-Three___ ___WILLIAM A. RINEHART, LOCI #141-525___ Attempted Breaking & Entering and Carrying a Concealed Weapon was convicted of the crimes of and sentenced by said Court to imprisonment in the ___London Correctional Institution___ for a term of ___1-15 years, suspended and placed on probation___; and

Whereas, the Parole Board, by ___unanimous___ vote ___eight (8) members participating (8-0) has recommended that the sentence be pardoned.___

Therefore, by virtue of the authority vested in the Governor by the Constitution and laws of this State, I do hereby direct that the said sentence of ___WILLIAM A. RINEHART, LOCI #141-525___ be ___pardoned___ as aforesaid. And of your execution of this warrant you will make due return without delay.

In Testimony Whereof, I have hereunto subscribed my name and caused the Great Seal of the State of Ohio to be affixed, at Columbus, this ___28th___ day of ___March___ in the year of our Lord, one thousand nine hundred and ___Ninety-Four___.

By the Governor:

SEALING OF THE RECORD OF CONVICTION

§2953.32

(A) First offender may apply to the sentencing court if convicted in the state, or to a court of common pleas if convicted in another state or in a federal court, for the sealing of the record of his conviction, at the expiration of three (3) years after his final discharge if convicted of a felony, or at the end of one year after his final discharge if convicted of a misdemeanor.

(B) (A hearing will be set, the D.A. can object, and a probation officer will investigate your case.)

(C) (1) The court shall do each of the following:
    (a) Determine if (you) are a first offender.
    (b) See if you have any pending charges.
    (c) Decide if (you) are rehabilitated to the satisfaction of the court.
    (d) If D.A. has objected, see why.
    (e) Weigh the interests of the applicant (in having your record sealed, against the needs of the government.

2.) If the court determines that (you) have met all of the above criteria, the court shall order all official records pertaining to his conviction sealed, and all index references deleted (erased). The proceedings in the case shall be deemed not to have occurred and the conviction shall be sealed.

(When the conviction is considered to have never happened, then you have regained your right to bear arms.)

EXPUNGEMENT OF RECORD AFTER BAIL FORFEITURE

§2953.42 (Misdemeanors)

(A) Any person who has been arrested for any misdemeanor and has agreed to forfeit bail, may apply to the court for an expungement of the record (erase or destroy the records). The application may be made at any time after one (1) year after the date of the bail forfeiture.

(B) —the court shall set a hearing, and notify the prosecuting authority— and if there are no pending cases, the court shall dismiss the charges and order that all records pertaining to the case be expunged. (All information in the case shall be destroyed) and the proceedings in the case shall be deemed as to never have happened. (In turn giving you no criminal record).

SEALING OF OFFICIAL RECORDS AFTER NOT GUILTY FINDING, DISMISSAL OF PROCEEDINGS, OR NO BILL

§ 2953.52.

(A) 1. Any person who is found not guilty of an offense by a jury or a court or who is named as the defendant in a dismissed complaint, indictment or information may apply (immediately) to the court for an order to seal the record in the case.

2. Any person against whom a no bill is entered (by a jury) after 2 years of the no bill for sealing of the records.

The court shall (investigate the case) and if the interests of the person having the record outweigh the government interests, the court shall order that all official records be sealed and–
– the proceedings in the case be deemed as to never have occurred. (Sealing of the records in this case is for felonies or serious misdemeanors-but it still restores your right to bear arms-in the courts. You never lost them if the charges were dropped.)

As in other states, Ohio allows you the filing of motions for free, if you are poor or broke, (indigent). Be aware that every case in which there is a motion for sealing or expungement (erasure of the records) there will be an in-depth investigation done on you by the prosecutor, the probation department, and law enforcement. Also, be aware that you will need to have a copy of the court proceedings with every motion you file. To file-go to or call the court and ask for a sample case or actual case that has been decided already and write your motion exactly like that, using your name, of course.

CORRECTING YOUR CRIMINAL RECORD

If you look at my criminal record on page 107, you will see that on the FBI file appears PD, Dayton, Ohio, 8-13-73, B&E; CCW, convicted of B&E at night, 5 years probation. Then, on down the page, appears Corr Inst, (Correctional Institute), Chillicothe, Ohio, 4-1-75, B&E at night, 1-15 years (in the penitentiary).

Now, if you keep looking, the one at the top has two numbers, SID A 556 204, 42561 and SID A 556 204. The SID is the State Identification Number.

The other one has the number, A 141-525, at the Chillicothe Correctional Institute.

Here's the problem, they are the same case!

Any law enforcement people that saw this record, and there were more than a few, had to believe that I committed two felonies in Ohio, one in 1973, and another in 1975.

Believe me, mistakes like this can kill you-but, keep looking. Notice on the Louisiana state police record that the file is much longer, it has numerous misdemeanors, but look again at the felony convictions, first page and, you will see the same thing that's on the FBI rap sheet. Again, from the looks of it, I had two felonies in Ohio, one in '73, and one in '75. And, again, they are the same one. That extra felony has been on my criminal record for almost twenty years, and I didn't realize it-until I started clearing my own record.

And, again, almost twenty years later, I had to file a motion in the courts of Ohio to prove that I was right. The problem arose when nobody wanted to take responsibility for it. Obviously, there are two felony records. Obviously, I went to prison. But, I finally figured out what had happened. When I was arrested in 1973, the Dayton, Ohio police department reported the arrest to the FBI, as well they should have. And that was when I was placed on probation. But, when the probation was revoked, and I was sent to the penitentiary, the state took it upon themselves to report the record again to the FBI.

And, that caused some problems. It meant, unless I could prove otherwise, I was a Three-Time-Loser! I could go to prison for my natural life if I ever got into trouble again.

So, I had an Ohio Criminal Codes book mailed to me, and started on the relief from disability motion, while I was still working on the full pardon, and expungement. While going through the book, I found a tiny little section entitled: Rule 36, Clerical Mistakes.

Quickly, I wrote up a motion to correct the criminal record, and have that extra felony removed. I figured things were bad enough the way they were. The following two pages show the result of my motion to correct. If I hadn't noticed it, the extra felony charge would still be there, but it shows what a little perseverance can do. The criminal records can be wrong, and they can be corrected.

IN THE COMMON PLEAS COURT OF MONTGOMERY COUNTY, OHIO
CRIMINAL DIVISION

STATE OF OHIO	:	CASE NO. 73-CR-1052
Plaintiff	:	(Judge Dodge)
- vs -	:	
WILLIAM ARTHUR RINEHART	:	ORDER CORRECTING THE RECORD
Defendant	:	

****

This cause came before the Court on Defendant's Motion for Correction of Defendant's Criminal Record. The Defendant's record with the Federal Bureau of Investigation is in error in that it appears that Defendant has two convictions for Breaking and Entering. See attached Exhibit "1". However, the Defendant had only one conviction in Montgomery County Common Pleas Court, Case Number 73-CR-1052.

IT IS HEREBY ORDERED, ADJUDGED AND DECREED that the record of Defendant, WILLIAM ARTHUR RINEHART, FBI Number 767 116F is in error, as it duplicates the conviction of Case Number 73-CR-1052. All Law Enforcement Agencies having any record of WILLIAM ARTHUR RINEHART are to change and correct that record to read that only one (1) felony conviction exists. Further, an Entry Granting Relief from Disability was Ordered by this Court in said case on May 14, 1992.

All agencies, including but not limited to the Federal Bureau of Investigation, the Ohio Department of Corrections, the City of Dayton Police Department, the Montgomery County Sheriff's Office, and the repositories of each agency are hereby ORDERED to correct their records of WILLIAM ARTHUR RINEHART to reflect that only one felony conviction exists in the State of Ohio.

SO ORDERED:

_____
JUDGE RICHARD S. DODGE

MATHIAS H. HECK, JR.
PROSECUTING ATTORNEY OF
MONTGOMERY COUNTY, OHIO

By _____
JANET R. SORRELL
Assistant Prosecuting Attorney
301 West Third Street
Suite 500
Dayton, Ohio 45402
(513) 225-5757

I hereby certify this to be a true and correct copy.
Witness my hand and seal this 6 day of _____ 1994

_____, Clerk
Clerk of Common Pleas
Court of Montgomery County, Ohio
By _____
Deputy

Ohio Firearm Rights Recovery

FEDERAL BUREAU OF INVESTIGATION
IDENTIFICATION DIVISION
WASHINGTON, D.C. 20537

5/7/91 CSSS/kjh

Use of the following FBI record, NUMBER 767 116 F , is REGULATED BY LAW. It is furnished FOR OFFICIAL USE ONLY and should ONLY BE USED FOR PURPOSE REQUESTED. When further explanation of arrest charge or disposition is needed, communicate directly with the agency that contributed the fingerprints.

CONTRIBUTOR OF FINGERPRINTS	NAME AND NUMBER	ARRESTED OR RECEIVED	CHARGE	DISPOSITION
PD Columbus OH	William Arthur Rinehart 102899	6-12-70	conv trust	6/19/70 dismissed
PD Dayton OH	William Arthur Rinehart 42561 SID A 556 204	8-13-73	B & E; CCW	Convicted of B & E at night 5 yrs probation
PD Nashville TN	William Arthur Rinhart 58014	2-13-75	flight to avoid prosecution - parole viol state OH 4902	TOT Ohio authorities
Corr Inst Chillicothe OH	William Arthur Rinehart A 141 525	4-1-75	B & E at night	1-15 yrs; 5-12-75 Trans to LPF susp sent 6-24-75 sect 2947.061 r,c Montgomery Co OH
PD Tucson AZ	William Arthur Rinehart 8001150281/ 1026260-M	1-15-80	agg Aslt on PO	Reduced to Misdemeanor (Class 1 Assault), warrant issued on 2-14-80, quashed on 4-15-81 as case was deemed to old to prosecute
PD Natchitoches LA	Bill Arthur Rinehart 8762	8-16-80	Simple Battery RS14:35	Withdrawn, Court Costs Paid

Clear Your Record and Own a Gun

1-4 (Rev. 7-19-77)

2

UNITED STATES DEPARTMENT OF JUSTICE
FEDERAL BUREAU OF INVESTIGATION
IDENTIFICATION DIVISION
WASHINGTON, D.C. 20537

5/7/91 CSSS/KJH

Use of the following FBI record, NUMBER   767 116 F   , is REGULATED BY LAW. It is furnished FOR OFFICIAL USE ONLY and should ONLY BE USED FOR PURPOSE REQUESTED. When further explanation of arrest charge or disposition is needed, communicate directly with the agency that contributed the fingerprints.

CONTRIBUTOR OF FINGERPRINTS	NAME AND NUMBER	ARRESTED OR RECEIVED	CHARGE	DISPOSITION
PD Lafayette LA	William Arthur Rinehart 14323 SID 935-740	5-29-83	Simple Burglary Carring a concealed weapon Sim. burglary of auto(2 cts)	
Dept Of Corr Lafayette LA	William Rinehart LFY #48797 SID 0935740	5-29-83 FP 8-15-86	simple battery DISMISSED	12/8/83- three yeras Parish Jail credit for time served (Clemency Investigation)
SO Lafayette LA	William A. Rinehart 96338	12-14-87	OWI 1st Expunged	LPCC

108

Chapter 8
Get Your Case in Court

Most of us have heard of the famous Writ Of Habeas Corpus, but few of us that are not in the legal profession have ever run across anything called a "Writ Of Mandamus". Mandamus is, by definition:

Mandamus, we command; a prerogative writ issued by a court, addressed to a natural person or corporation, and not to the sheriff (as a Writ of Habeas Corpus is), as are ordinary writs, requiring the person to whom it is addressed to do some act therein specified, which is generally one connected with his duty as a public official or as a corporation exercising public franchises. The writ may be alternative, i.e., show cause why he should not be compelled to do as he was ordered, or peremptory, after the final hearing, when there is nothing for the defendant to do but obey.

Mandamus is a civil action, for example, in Louisiana, in the Code of Civil Procedure:

Chapter 3, Article 3861, Mandamus, Definition

Mandamus is a writ directing a public officer (including judges) to perform any of the duties set forth –(includes court hearings for 'show cause' -why something should not be done as ordered. As in, you had a hearing date set by the court, and the court kept cancelling your date or never notified you of any hearing at all.)

Article 3862-Issuance of Mandamus

A writ of mandamus may be issued in all cases where the law provides no relief by ordinary means or where the delay obtained in ordinary relief may cause injustice.

Article 3863-Person against whom writ directed

A writ of mandamus may be directed to a public officer to compel the performance of a ministerial duty required by law--.

A writ of mandamus is directed to a public official, including judges, that has not followed through on a court order, or has ordered something that has never been enforced. In short, if you were to file a motion for expungement, or a motion for restoration of civil rights, or a motion for relief from disability, and the court of correct jurisdiction never set your motion for hearing, or a hearing date was set but continuously postponed, you have the option in filing a writ of mandamus-in other words, make the court tell you why. In most areas of law, this is called a "show cause" motion. It literally orders the court to have a hearing, and at that hearing show cause why your motions have not been heard, and if cause cannot be found, it will force the court to set a date and time so that your motion will be heard.

Remember, trying to regain your right to bear arms is a request, not a right. You don't want to make the court(s) mad at you for filing an unnecessary motion for mandamus-use this motion with caution, and sparingly. It should be a last resort.

The following pages consist of supplemental copies and evidence for previously filed writ of mandamus by the author.

GET YOUR CASE IN COURT

IN THE

SUPREME COURT OF THE STATE OF LOUISIANA

NEW ORLEANS, LOUISIANA

WILLIAM A. RINEHART	*	DOCKET NO.
Plaintiff	*	STATE OF LOUISIANA
	*	NEW ORLEANS, LOUISIANA
VERSUS	*	
	*	
BUREAU OF CRIMINAL RECORDS	*	
STATE OF LOUISIANA	*	
BATON ROUGE, LOUISIANA	*	

****

SUPPLEMENTAL COPIES AND EVIDENCE FOR PREVIOUSLY
FILED WRIT OF MANDAMUS

MAY IS PLEASE THIS HONORABLE COURT:

The Mover in the above action, William A. Rinehart, now submits these 8 copies of his Writ of Mandamus and evidence of his cause of action, with the respect and prayerfully requests that this Court please excuse his lack of the legal profession, in that he did not submit the proper number of

111

copies originally. In addition to the 8 copies, Mover now presents, with explanations, the evidence of wrongdoing on the part of the State Bureau of Criminal Identification, located in Baton Rouge, Louisiana.

It is the contention of the Mover that he has an existing record with this Bureau of Criminal Records, even though his <u>single</u> Louisiana felony record was ordered <u>expunged</u>, twice, by Order of the 15th Judicial District Court. Further, he contends that his record should have been erased in 1988, but through this Honorable Supreme Court, he brought the expungement back to light in 1992, because the State Police and F.B.I. had refused to expunge his record. Again, by remand through this Supreme Court, and the 3rd Circuit Court of Appeals, the 15th Judicial District Court Ordered the expungement of his record.

EVIDENCE

1. Letter from Bureau of Criminal Identification-Louisiana State Police, Lt. M. Futch, stating that expungment is not permitted under <u>present</u> <u>Statutes.</u> Mover states that although that may certainly be possible, his Orders of Expungment date to 1988 and 1992. Certainly, these legal and valid Orders are retroactive to those dates, and should have been enforced then-but even so, they are still just as legal, and should be enforced according to the laws then. Notice that the date on this letter is June 21, 1994.

2. The second document is an Order To Expunge the Mover's Louisiana single felony, dated December 14, 1988, signed by the Honorable Judge Benny Gautreaux, (now retired). Please notice that this Order is under L.S.A. 44:9, and contains the words <u>destroy all records.</u> Mover contends that his record with the State Police and Bureau of Criminal Records should have been expunged then-but remained in existence, despite the Order.

3. The third document is a copy of the 15th Judicial District's report on all criminal records in existence at this time, (certified copy obtained September 6, 1994). The Mover has absolutely **no criminal record** in existence, as evidenced by this document.

4. The fourth document is yet another Order of Expungement, by the Honorable Judge Michot, 15th Judicial District, State of Louisiana. This Order was obtained through the 3rd Circuit and Supreme Court on Remand. Please notice the explicitness of the Order-<u>State Police</u> and F.B.I.

5. Document number 5 is a front page of the 'rap' sheet of the <u>current</u> record of the Mover, from the Louisiana State Police, with Document number 6 showing that the State Police having plainly disregarded the Orders of 2 District Judges, and have retained and illegally disseminated his <u>expunged</u> record at will.

6. Document number 6 is the front page of a Motion To Dismiss a case the Mover has in Federal District Court against the State of Louisiana-brought by the State. Please notice, the second page, document number 7, as a part of this Motion To Dismiss, that the State contends that the Mover not only has "one" felony conviction in Lafayette, but that he has **four (4)** felony convictions in Lafayette. Clearly, that is misinformation to a Federal Judge, as proven herein, by the Certified Statement of the Clerk of Court, Criminal Records, 15th Judicial District Court, Lafayette, Louisiana.

During a telephone conversation with the Bureau of Criminal Records Bureau, the Mover was told that that Agency may not be bound by a Judge's Order to Expunge his record, (Mr. Mike Baron, Attorney, Legal Section, B.C.I.). At this time, and under the laws of Louisiana Revised Statute 44:9, as of 1988, (the Original Order To Expunge), the Mover requests that this Honorable Supreme Court Order the Defendant(s) in this case, the Louisiana State Police, through the Bureau of Criminal Identification, Baton Rouge, Louisiana, on Writ of Mandamus, (or Certiorari, which may be fitting in this case), to explain to this Honorable Court, and the Mover, why these Orders to Expunge were and are adamantly ignored, without the Proper Authority to do so, and this Court Order that the Louisiana State Police and the Bureau of Criminal Identification be Ordered by this Court, to Expunge Mover's Louisiana FELONY conviction from

Get Your Case in Court

his record, as Ordered in 1988, and in 1992, with the proper safeguard mechanisms in place to assure compliance.

RESPECTFULLY SUBMITTED,

William A. Rinehart

WILLIAM A. RINEHART, Pro Se, Pauper
300 Spruce Dr., #204
Lafayette, Louisiana
70506
(318) 984-6046

Clear Your Record and Own a Gun

Chapter 9
Influence, How to Use It

In 1991, after being turned down for a full pardon twice before, I went to another hearing. At this hearing, I made my statements, answered the questions of the board, and found out later that they had voted unanimously to give me a full pardon, with the right to own, possess, receive, and transport firearms. The recommendation of the board went to the governor's office for signing. The governor of Louisiana at that time was Buddy Roemer. The recommendation had lain on his desk for three months before I became worried. At the end of six months, I became angry. At the end of nine months, I knew that something was wrong. An election year was coming up, and I suspected that Roemer didn't want to make any waves with his constituents–he was running for another term. I had no way of putting any pressure on the governor, except to keep calling his staff to check on the status of my pardon. I was told that it was among the stack of 700 or so on his desk awaiting action.

Roemer was running against the previous governor, Edwards, and figured he had no problems. Edwards had been known to grant pardons to rehabilitated ex-cons, and Roemer wanted to be different. (During one Edwards administration, the Chairman of the Board, Marsellis, was caught and convicted of selling pardons under the table.). I had been turned down twice before during Edwards' other two administrations.

True to form, Roemer waited until after he had lost the election to Edwards to start signing pardons. And when he did, and I got it in the mail, he had granted me a full pardon, with all civil rights, except the right to bear arms. The pardon would do me no good. The record had already been erased, but I wanted the pardon for my own personal satisfaction.

I met an attorney I kind of knew, Max Jordan, in the halls of the courthouse. He told me he was going to run for state senator, and asked that I support him. The election was only weeks away. I told Max about what Roemer had done to my pardon. He told me to get the paper work together and bring it to him. I did that, but in the meantime I told everybody I knew, and I know a few, to vote for Max. I went to campaign parties, put on bumper stickers, made a very small cash donation, and was on his list of volunteers.

Max won the election. I took the papers to him. He said he would talk to Governor Edwards. I told him I had heard that story before.

Max took the pardon to Governor Edwards. Edward's staff called me and told me to contact an attorney in Alexandria, La., and I called. Edwards' staff had already called this attorney, Camille Gravelle, and Gravelle said he had some papers for me. He faxed them to the Office Depot in Lafayette. I looked at the papers and was surprised–it was a re-submission of the pardon board's vote to the now new governor. I copied the motion, and took it to Max. Max saw Governor Edwards and explained the problem. By April 14, 1992, I had a full pardon, with the right to bear arms.

Later, Max's house burned in Lafayette, and I went over to help out. I thought it was the least I could do. He had kept his word–I had kept mine.

I had accomplished two things, I had my full pardon, and now I had a friend in the state senate that I knew I could trust.

I wondered if that kind of operation would work in other areas–support and trust a candidate, then ask for their help afterwards. I hadn't known it at the time, but that's the way it's always been done. It did work, and I accomplished a lot.

Sometimes it was a little on the sneaky side–I supported the candidates I pretty well knew would win, then supported the others–just in case. No bumper stickers on my car, no signs in my yard, but ready to go do whatever was called for. No matter who won, I could say that I had supported them, and ask for a favor. You can do that, too. Local judges, sheriffs, city councilmen/women, police chiefs, anyone that you know or think is or will be in a position to help your cause. Same with the state congressmen/women, state representatives, even governors. A little support can go a long, long way. Make sure they remember you. Don't be obvious about what you're doing. Play the field. It works.

You can also do the same thing with people that are not into politics–volunteer for organizations that help other people–Boys & Girls Clubs, VITA, YMCA, Red Cross, etc., and then, when you need a written recommendation, ask for one.

Get the impression that you have to do whatever it takes? You're right–you have to do what you have to do to get where you want to go. Education, working with kids, the poor, the illiterate, mixed with the elite of the political power, can get you almost anywhere.

Chapter 10
Filing Your Papers for Free

The court system in the United States cannot block you from filing your papers, motions, post-conviction relief requests, evidence of rehabilitation, etc, just because you can't pay the court costs. The justice system demands equality to all, not just those with a fat wallet. The concept of forma paupers (that point in life where there is no money) and the allowing of free access to the courts holds true in all of them, federal, state, city, or other. Just as when you're in court and you are asked if you can afford an attorney and you say no, the clerk of court where you are filing will want money when you file your papers, and you tell them you don't have any, but the papers need to be filed.

Almost every court I've been in, and was doing my own work without an attorney, I didn't have the money to file the papers I wanted to present to the clerk. So, the very first motion I filed was a motion to proceed in forma pauperis (sometimes called other things). It's a motion that states to the court that you do not have the money to pay for filing, but you need to access the court. Judges look at the motion and see if you're earning enough to pay for filing fees. If not, you can do it for free. First, you need to prove that you're broke, then get an affidavit from someone else that knows you that will say you're broke, and file that with the papers being signed by a notary public, with clerk of court. The judge will then issue an order that you can file your papers and motions for free. Most courts have their own forma pauperis forms to give you to fill out and bring back-with instructions included. After you have been granted forma pauperis status, then you can file all of your papers in that court without costs.

It is apparent that you can file for a presidential pardon and restoration of civil rights without fees. (There is a $17.00 fee for a copy of your FBI file).

In California, you can file for the certificate of rehabilitation and pardon at no costs, under Penal Code 1203.4, and 4852.01.

In Ohio, you request the form necessary to fill out to proceed in forma pauperis and return it to the clerk of court.

In Louisiana, you request a form to fill out, proving that you are indigent, and return it to the clerk of court.

In any case, in any court, in any federal, state or city or county court, you have the right to represent yourself, [Faretta v. California, (1975) 422 US 806, 45 L Ed 2d 562, 95 S Ct 2525]. This case also involves the quality of counsel. Also, in any court, you can still seek relief from disability, even if you have no money.

Epilog

Between the covers of this book, I have given you numerous ways of restoring your right to bear arms. Most certainly, I haven't covered all of them. Restraints on space and research forbid such an undertaking. However, it is the purpose of what is in here to give you an idea of what to look for wherever you are, and how to go about finding and using what you need.

In the Unites States, the right to bear arms is sacred–it seems almost unpatriotic to not have that oldest and most important right to defend ourselves and our families and property. The government is becoming more and more police-state minded, and if we're not careful, we are going to be a nation of people that have all of these constitutional rights, but they will have no meaning, and serve no purpose. They will be useless, but will look good on paper.

Criminal conduct certainly deserves to be recognized, and punished. Does that mean that the government should not recognize rehabilitation and act on it? Certainly not! For those of us that have made mistakes that were crimes, and there are more than a few of us, we understand that we did wrong, and paid the price. Some of us, like myself, as patriotic as anyone else that cried when Kennedy died, felt as if not only had our right to bear arms been ripped out of our lives when sentenced, but as if we had been left outside of our own country, looking in.

Some of us, such as myself, who have worn the uniform of the U. S. Army, and wore it proudly, were in shock when the gavel banged at the judge's bench and we could no longer have weapons in our homes to protect our own families' lives. For me, it was the saddest day in my life. If the court had known that pain, they may have thought that was punishment enough.

Truly, it has saddened me greatly to learn, in the writing of this book, to find that there are at least twelve states that have no procedure for restoring civil rights. But, they certainly have thousands of procedures for removing them.

In a society that has gone from respecting and defending civil liberties to removing and abstaining from the return of these rights, we have lost something near and dear to our hearts. We send our young men to other countries to fight for liberty and justice of freedom, but we cannot protect our own front yards. The following states have the legal power to arrest, convict, and sentence, but do not have the legal procedures in their state constitutions to restore the suspended rights removed by that conviction: Arkansas, Indiana, Kentucky, Maryland, Missouri, New Jersey, Oklahoma, Pennsylvania, Rhode Island, Texas, Vermont, and Virginia. Yes, the same Pennsylvania where Philadelphia is, where the Declaration of Independence was signed, on July 4, 1776; Virginia, where George Washington lived, New Jersey, where three of the signers of the U.S. Constitution resided, and the list of Forefathers goes on and on. What were these states doing when their own constitutions were being written? Apparently, forgiveness was not in the forefront of their thoughts. Civil rights, so easily taken away, but no laws to return them.

Bearing arms is a serious business, but in these days a necessity. It is true that if all the rights to bear arms are taken away from society, then the only ones to have guns will be the police and outlaws. And we're almost a police state now. I sincerely hope that I have helped restore some rights. The battle for rehabilitation, and the recognition of it, rages on. Don't give up. Make yourself count. Don't let our country self-destruct.

GLOSSARY

APPEAL– an application to a higher court to correct or modify the judgement of a lower court. The person initiating (doing) the appeal is called an appellant, or petitioner, the other side is called the appellees, or respondents.

APPEARANCE– going in front of the judge at court.

AUTOMATIC PARDON– there are some states that grant Pardons to Defendants automatically on release from incarceration or probation, especially for First Offenses. It restores all Rights that were lost. See if your state has such a law.

CLERK OF COURT– these are the people than run the system. It is with them that you will deal with when you are filing any papers for the court. Most of the time, they are willing to help you.

CRIMINAL DIVISION– make sure that you go to the right place in the court when you are filing any papers-don't take Criminal Division papers to a Civil Division clerk for filing. They won't accept them. Criminal Division is also where you go to get copies of your case-the Minutes.

Glossary

COURT MINUTES– a written document that states exactly what happened to you in court-it has the charge(s), date, sentence, and docket number, along with the names of the judge and everyone that was in the courtroom that day. You <u>need</u> a copy of this document.

DOCKET NUMBER– this is the number given to your case for tracking and finding your file. It will appear on every court document that has anything to do with you.

DISABILITY– having a criminal record <u>disables</u> you from having the Right To Bear Arms. (As in Relief From Disability).

EXPUNGE– expungement; to erase, strike out, destroy.

FELONY– a more serious criminal charge, felonies are usually considered as crimes that the sentence was or could have been a term in jail or prison for a year or more.

FILING– the act of taking or mailing your parers, motions, evidence, etc, to the court for acceptance of stamp and the papers become a part of the case. (All Motion must be filed).

INDIGENT– poor

JURISDICTION– any state motions for state Relief from Disability must be filed with the court within the bounds of where the Hearing must take place. File State motions in State courts, City Motions in City courts, Federal Motions in Federal Courts, etc.

HEARING– the act of the court hearing motions and evidence and making a Ruling (decision).

LIMITS– every court has certain limits to its judicial jurisdiction. Every case has a time limit in which motions and hearings must take place after filing.

Glossary

MOTIONS– the act of writing a formal document and presenting it to the court, or a verbal motion done in court, directed to the judge.

MISDEMEANORS– cases that are minor in range, usually a fine and/or a short jail sentence are induced. Less than a Felony. (Misdemeanors do not suspend or revoke your Right To Bear Arms).

NOLLE PROSEQUI– a case that is decided not to be prosecuted, the charges are dropped, or dismissed. Does not erase the arrest record.

PARDON– the act of restoring all Civil Rights to a person after a conviction, either by a state's governor in state jurisdiction, or the President of the U.S. in Federal jurisdiction. It is an act of forgiveness, not a legal right, and done on request, not demand.

POST-CONVICTION RELIEF– any action that lessens the stigma or consequences of having a criminal record-pardon, parole, Relief From Disability, dismissal of prosecution, sealing of the records, restoration of Rights, etc., are considered to be post-conviction relief.

PROBATION– the act of being released after being sentenced, on good behavior, on a specified length of time. Can be supervised or unsupervised. Some states have statutes that restore Civil Rights at the completion of Probation. Probation is a chance to make good and rehabilitate-and start a new life.

REHABILITATION– 1. the act of restoring a handicapped (as in having a criminal record) a person to a useful life through education and therapy. 2. to reinstate the good name of---. 3. to restore the former rank, privileges or rights of---. 4. to restore to former to a former condition (as in possession of all Civil Rights.)

Glossary

RESTORATION OF RIGHTS– regaining all civil rights as pertaining to the Constitution of the United States singular, and the Constitution of each state under its own Constitution, with state jurisdiction, as in Right To Vote, Right To Bear Arms, etc.

TIME– as in the waiting period before you can apply for the Restoration of Citizenship Rights.

VENUE– that court that has jurisdiction over your case, whether it be Federal, State, County or City. For seeking Post Conviction Relief, you must apply in the court where your records are and you went to court.

WRITTEN MOTIONS– use the exact form of written motions that each court uses-you can get a copy of one from the Clerk of Court, and follow that exactly in making your own motion, i.e., Motion To Set Aside Conviction, Motion To Dismiss, Motion to Expunge, Motion For Certificate of Rehabilitation, etc.

WRIT– as in Writ of Mandamus- a written court order for a judicial process-a legal document demanding something of the court, (as in Writ of Habeas Corpus).

SOURCES

LAW

CALIFORNIA PENAL CODE-West Pub. Co., Official Classification, 1994 Edition

CALIFORNIA CODE OF CIVIL PROCEDURE-West Pub. Co. Official Classification, 1994 Edition

OHIO CRIMINAL LAW HANDBOOK, 7th Annual Ed., Covering Title 29, the Ohio Criminal Code, Anderson Pub. Co.

UNITED STATES CODE, ANNOTATED, TITLE 18.

WEST'S LOUISIANA STATUTORY CRIMINAL LAW AND PROCEDURE-West

LOUISIANA CIVIL CODE-West

United States Justice Department

United States Treasury Department-Bureau of Alcohol, Tobacco, and Firearms

CONSTITUTIONAL LAW DESKBOOK-Individual Rights-
Lawyer's Co-operative Pub. Co.

THE LAW DICTIONARY- Anderson Pub. Co.

U. S. Department of Justice-Probation/Parole

OTHER

Office of the Governor-State of California

Office of the Governor-State of Louisiana

Office of the Governor-State of Ohio

Department of Probation-Federal Courthouse-
Lafayette, La.

National Institute of Justice-Washington, D.C.

THE AMERICAN HERITAGE DICTIONARY-
Houghton Mifflin Co.,Boston

WEBSTER'S NEW WORLD DICTIONARY-The Southwestern
Co., Tenn.

"HOW TO CLEAR YOUR CRIMINAL RECORD",
Flores Pub. Co.-Miami

15th Judicial District Court, Lafayette, La.

19th Judicial District Court, Baton Rouge, La.

3rd Circuit Court of Appeals, Baton Rouge, La.

Senator/Attorney Lomax Jordan, Lafayette/Baton Rouge, La.

U.S. District Court, Western District of Louisiana

Sources

The Supreme Court of Louisiana

Louisiana Department of Probation/Parole

Common Pleas Court, Montgomery County, Dayton, Ohio

The CONSTITUTION of the United States of America

The Supreme Court Reporter

The Author

The author, W.A. Rinehart, sold his first "How To" book to *Entreprenuer* magazine, How To Start Your Own Lawyer Referral Service", a national monthly publication, in 1990.

Immediately after that publication, he began writing short story fiction for the Regal Publishing Co., New Jersey, and has been published over twenty times. Among the titles: "What Comes Around Goes Around", "On A Hill-Far Away", "When My Ship Comes In", and others.

In 1994, his book, "How To Clear Your Criminal Record" was published and distributed by Flores Publishing Co., (ISBN 0-918751-41-1) under William Rinehart. Flores holds another contract for the book, "How To File Your Own Law Suit", due out in 1995.

Rinehart has been published on request by the Louisiana Bar Association, (on the 6th Amendment, 'Right To A Fair Trial' in celebration of the Bicentennial of the Bill Of Rights).

He holds a bachelor of science degree in criminal justice from the University of Southwestern Louisiana, has attended Law School in California, and grad school at the University of Southern Mississippi, the People's Law School in Lafayette, and paralegal studies taught by the School of Paralegal Studies, Professional Career Development Institute, Atlanta, Georgia, (Honors Program).

He has been presented awards in investigations, Outstanding College Students of America, and Award of Merit by the Knights of Columbus.

He has been a corrections officer at the Louisiana state penitentiary at Angola, Louisiana, and an armed tower guard at the Hunt Corrections Center, St. Gabriel, Louisiana, 1990-91.

In 1985, when he started to college at Southwest Louisiana, he had two criminal felony records and many misdemeanor records to deal with before he graduated, one of them in Ohio.

By 1992, after taking time out to be a state corrections officer,

Rinehart had expunged (erased) the Louisiana felony record, twice, had it pardoned, twice, and in Ohio, he had been given a full pardon and had received a relief from the disability of that felony record, with a restoration of all civil rights. As a result of those court actions, he has the legal right to buy, sell, own, trade or transport weapons anywhere in the United States.

Having been an optical lab tech, a chef, a steward on the high seas, an electrician, a cook for the gold camps in Nome, Alaska, an inmate and a guard, he sometimes compares himself with the western writer, Louis L'amour. His desire is to help others by writing about what he has done. He welcomes mail and ideas.

Notes

Notes

Notes

Other Books Available From Desert Publications

01/10/95

001	Firearms Silencers Volume 1	$9.95
003	The Silencer Cookbook	$9.95
004	Select Fire Uzi Modification Manual	$9.95
005	Expedient Hand Grenades	$13.95
007	007 Travel Kit, The	$8.00
008	Law Enforcement Guide to Firearms Silencer	$8.95
009	Springfield Rifle, The	$11.95
010	Full Auto Vol 3 MAC-10 Mod Manual	$7.95
012	Fighting Garand, The	$11.95
013	M1 Carbine Owners Manual	$9.95
014	Ruger Carbine Cookbook	$8.00
015	M-14 Rifle, The	$8.95
016	AR-15, M16 and M16A1 5.56mm Rifles	$11.95
017	Shotguns	$11.95
019	AR15 A2/M16A2 Assault Rifle	$8.95
022	Full Auto Vol 7 Bingham AK-22	$7.95
027	Full Auto Vol 4 Thompson SMG	$7.95
030	STANAG Mil-Talk	$12.95
031	Thompson Submachine Guns	$13.95
033	H&R Reising Submachine Gun Manual	$12.95
035	How to Build Silencers	$6.95
036	Full Auto Vol 2 Uzi Mod Manual	$7.95
049	Firearm Silencers Vol 3	$13.95
050	Firearm Silencers Vol 2	$16.95
054	Company Officers HB of Ger. Army	$11.95
056	German Infantry Weapons Vol 1	$14.95
058	Survival Armory	$27.95
060	Survival Gunsmithing	$9.95
061	FullAuto Vol 1 Ar-15 Mod Manual	$7.95
064	HK Assault Rifle Systems	$27.95
065	SKS Type of Carbines, The	$14.95
066	Private Weaponeer, The	$9.95
067	Rough Riders, The	$24.95
068	Lasers & Night Vision Devices	$29.95
069	Ruger P-85 Family of Handguns	$11.95
071	Dirty Fighting	$11.95
072	Live to Spend It	$29.95
073	Military Ground Rappelling Techniques	$11.95
074	Smith & Wesson Autos	$27.95
080	German MG-34 Machinegun Manual	$9.95
081	Crossbows: From 35 Years With the Weapon	$11.95
082	Op. Man. 7.62mm M24 Sniper Weapon	$7.95
083	USMC AR-15/M-16 A2 Manual	$16.95
084	Urban Combat	$21.95
085	Caching Techniques of U.S. Army Special Forces	$9.95
086	US Marine Corps Essential Subjects	$16.95
087	The L'il M-1, The .30 Cal. M-1 Carbine	$14.95
088	Concealed Carry Made Easy	$14.95
089	Apocalypse Tomorrow	$17.95
090	M14 and M14A1 Rifles and Rifle Marksmanship	$16.95
091	Crossbow As a Modern Weapon	$11.95
092	MP40 Machinegun	$11.95
093	Map Reading and Land Navigation	$19.95
094	U. S. Marine Corps Scout/Sniper Training Manual	$16.95
095	Clear Your Record & Own a Gun	$14.95
096	Sig/Sauer Handguns	$16.95
097	Poor Man's Nuclear Bomb	$19.95
099	Poor Man's Sniper Rifle	$14.95
100	Submachine Gun Designers Handbook	$14.95
101	Lock Picking Simplified	$8.50
102	Combination Lock Principles	$7.95
103	How to Fit Keys by Impressioning	$8.95
104	Keys To Understanding Tubular Locks	$8.00
105	Techniques of Safe & Vault Manipulation	$9.95
106	Lockout -Techniques of Forced Entr	$11.95
107	Bugs Electronic Surveillance	$10.00
110	Improvised Weapons of Amer. Underground	$10.00
111	Training Handbook of the American Underground	$10.00
114	FullAuto Vol 8 M14A1 & Mini 14	$7.95
116	Handbook Bomb Threat/Search Procedures	$8.00
117	Improvised Lock Picks	$10.00
119	Fitting Keys By Reading Locks	$7.00
120	How to Open Handcuffs Without Keys	$7.95
121	Electronic Locks Volume 1	$8.00
122	With British Snipers, To the Reich	$24.95
125	Browning Hi-Power Pistols	$9.95
126	P-08 Parabellum Luger Auto Pistol	$9.95
127	Walther P-38 Pistol Manual	$9.95
128	Colt .45 Auto Pistol	$8.95
129	Beretta - 9MM M9	$8.95
130	FullAuto Vol 5 M1 Carbine to M2	$7.95
133	FN-FAL Auto Rifles	$10.00
135	AK-47 Assault Rifle	$10.00
136	UZI Submachine Gun	$8.00
140	Sten Submachine Gun, The	$8.00
200	Fighting Back on the Job	$10.00
202	Secret Codes & Ciphers	$9.95
204	Improvised Munitions Black Book Vol 1	$12.95
206	Improvised Munitions Black Book Vol 2	$12.95
207	CIA Field Exp Preparation of Black Powder	$8.95
208	CIA Field Exp. Meth/Explo. Preparat	$8.95
209	CIA Improvised Sabotage Devices	$12.00
210	CIA Field Exp. Incendiary Manual	$12.00
211	Science of Revolutionary Warfare	$9.95
212	Agents HB of Black Bag Ops.	$12.95
214	Electronic Harassment	$10.00
217	Improvised Rocket Motors	$6.95
218	Impro. Munitions/Ammonium Nitrate	$7.50
219	Improvised Batteries/Det. Devices	$8.95
220	Impro. Expolo/Use In Deton. Devices	$7.95
221	Evaluation of Imp Shaped Charges	$8.95
222	American Tools of Intrigue	$12.00
225	Impro. Munitions Black Book Vol 3	$21.95
226	Poor Man's James Bond Vol 2	$21.95
227	Explosives and Propellants	$10.00
229	Select Fire 10/22	$10.00
230	Poor Man's James Bond Vol 1	$21.95
231	Assorted Nasties	$19.95
234	L.A.W. Rocket System	$8.00
240	Clandestine Ops Man/Central America	$9.95
241	Mercenary Operations Manual	$9.95
250	Improvised Shaped Charges	$8.95
251	Two Component High Exp. Mixtures	$9.95
260	Survival Evasion & Escape	$13.95
262	Infantry Scouting, Patrol, & Sniping	$11.95
263	Engineer Explosives of WWI	$7.95
300	Brown's Alcohol Motor Fuel Cookbook	$11.95
301	How to Build a Junkyard Still	$10.00
303	Alcohol Distillers Handbook	$14.95
306	Brown's Book of Carburetors	$11.95
310	MAC-10 Cookbook	$9.95
350	Cheating At Cards	$12.00
367	Brown's Lawsuit Cookbook	$14.95
400	Hand to Hand Combat	$9.50
401	USMC Hand to Hand Combat	$7.95
402	US Marine Bayonet Training	$8.95
404	Camouflage	$10.00
409	Guide to Germ Warfare	$10.00
410	Emergency War Surgery	$21.95
411	Homeopathic First Aid	$9.95
412	Defensive Shotgun	$12.95
414	Hand to Hand Combat by D'Eliscue	$7.95
415	999 Survived	$6.00
416	Sun, Sand & Survival	$6.00
420	USMC Sniping	$13.95
424	Prisons Bloody Iron	$10.95
425	Napoleon's Maxims of War	$9.95
429	Invisible Weapons/Modern Ninja	$10.00
432	Cold Weather Survival	$11.95
435	Homestead Carpentry	$10.00
436	Construction Secret Hiding Places	$8.95
437	US Army Survival	$24.95
438	Survival Shooting for Women	$11.95
442	Survival Medicine	$10.00
443	Can You Survive	$10.00
444	Canteen Cup Cookery	$7.95
445	Leadership Handbook of Small Unit Ops	$11.95
447	Vigilante Handbook	$11.95
448	Shootout II	$11.95
453	Catalog of Military Suppliers	$11.95
454	Survival Childbirth	$8.95
455	Police Karate	$10.95
456	Survival Guns	$21.95
457	Water Survival Training	$5.95
470	Emergency Medical Care/Disaster	$11.95
500	Guerilla Warfare	$10.00
503	Irregular Forces	$8.95
504	Ranger Training & Operations	$14.95
507	Spec. Forces Demolitions Trng HB	$16.95
510	IRA Handbook	$9.95
511	Battlefield Analysis/Inf. Weapons	$9.95
512	US Army Bayonet Training	$9.95
542	Desert Storm Wept. Recog. Guide	$9.95
543	Professional Homemade Car Bomb	$10.00
544	Combat Loads for Sniper Rifles	$12.00
551	Take My Gun..If You Dare	$10.95
552	Aunt Bessie's Wood Stove Cookbook	$7.50
605	Jackedup & Ripped off	$10.00
610	Trapping & Destruc. of Exec. Cars	$10.00
C-002	How To Open A Swiss Bank Account	$5.95
C-011	Defending Your Retreat	$7.95
C-019	How To Become A Class 3 MG Dealer	$3.95
C-020	Methods of Long Term Storage	$7.95
C-021	How To Obtain Gun Dealer Licenses	$3.95
C-022	Confid. Gun Dealers Guide/Whlesler	$2.50
C-023	Federal Firearms Laws	$4.50
C-028	Militarizing the Mini-14	$8.95
C-029	Combat History of the M-1 Carbine	$6.95
C-030	OSS/CIA Assassination Device	$4.00
C-038	How To Build A Beer Can Morter	$4.95
C-040	Criminal Use of False ID	$11.95
C-051	Surviving Doomsday	$11.95
C-052	CIA Explosives for Sabotage	$9.00
C-058	Brass Knuckle Bible	$7.95
C-080	USA Urban Survival Arsenal	$7.95
C-099	Dead or Alive	$7.95
C-175	Elementary Field Interrogation	$14.95
C-176	Beat the Box	$7.95
C-177	Boobytraps	$8.00
C-209	Guide/Vietcong Boobytraps/Device	$8.00
C-386	Self-Defense Requires No Apology	$11.95
C-679	M16A1 Rifle Manual Cartoon Version	$6.95
9-9031	Become a Licensed Gun Collector	$4.95
FP-9	Micro Uzi Select Fire Mod Manual	$9.95

PRICES SUBJECT TO CHANGE WITHOUT NOTICE

Send $4.00 for a complete catalog
80 pages
Free with order

Send order to:
DESERT Publications
P.O. Box 1751 Dept. BK-095
El Dorado, AR 71730-1751 USA
501-862-2077

Add $4.95 to all orders for shipping & handling.